THE POET OF CHRISTMAS EVE

Courtesy of the New-York Historical Society

"Santa Claus" by Robert Walter Weir

The Poet of Christmas Eve

A LIFE OF CLEMENT CLARKE MOORE

1779 — 1863

By

SAMUEL WHITE PATTERSON

Morehouse-Gorham Co., New York

PRINTED IN THE UNITED STATES OF AMERICA
SOWERS PRINTING COMPANY, LEBANON, PENNSYLVANIA

To My Brother

ROBERT CAULDWELL PATTERSON

*in whose library-office I
first saw books from the
library of Clement C. Moore
and received the incentive
to study the life and work
of the Poet of Chelsea and
Christmas Eve*

and

To My Friend

EDMUND ASTLEY PRENTIS

*who in recent years has
revived my early interest
and encouraged the writing
of this book*

Preface

CLEMENT CLARKE MOORE deserves a full-length biography. He lived a significant life in a significant period of American history, the first eight decades after the Declaration of Independence. He was not an idle spectator during the first half of the nineteenth century, but associated himself with many good causes. Born to wealth, he did not fritter away his time in purposeless pursuits. He was more than the Poet of Christmas Eve, though it is on "A Visit from St. Nicholas" that his fame chiefly rests.

Moore was a scholar, a pamphleteer, a musician and patron of music, a churchman, a professor, and a college trustee as well as a poet. He spent a good part of his younger manhood trying to improve national conditions. He was all his life a citizen of his native New York, which was glad to honor him to the degree that his modesty permitted. He sought the quiet of his rural estate not far from the throbbing city, and pretended to be no other than himself. He shunned the limelight as best he could. He would probably dislike to see this book about him, and yet there is no need to apologize for it; he merited such recognition.

My interest in Clement C. Moore was stimulated by circumstances. I was born in Chelsea and heard of the Poet of Christmas Eve in earliest childhood. I was first seriously

attracted to him in my youth when I used to look through
the glass doors of a tall bookcase behind my brother's chair
in the Sunday school library at St. Peter's Church, not far
from the General Theological Seminary, where Dr. Moore
taught for over a quarter of a century. His son, Benjamin
Moore, had given the learned books to his friend, the rector, after the poet's death. I should like to add, parentheti-
cally, that I was born on Christmas Day, across the street
from St. Peter's Church, which Clement C. Moore did so
much to establish, and near the seminary he so long served.

In early manhood, I lectured on Clement C. Moore's life
and career and recited his famous poem at Christmastime.
The late Miss Louise Stephania Hopper, well-known minia-
turist and matron of the seminary, drew eight water colors
to illustrate "A Visit from St. Nicholas." I had them made
into slides for my annual talks and recitals.

My mother's family, the Maxwells, removed to Chelsea
in the 1840's and lived within a few blocks of Chelsea House,
Moore's residence, still on its high bluff above the river. In
the parish that he helped found I breathed the spirit he in-
fused. My older brothers, Dr. William Maxwell Patterson
and Robert Cauldwell Patterson, were Clement C. Moore's
successors as wardens, many years after his time. I was myself a vestryman.

At the time of my writing the centennial history of Chelsea
and its church, I enjoyed the benefit of the late William
Scoville Moore's interest, and quite recently of several members of his family, in the selection of cuts for this biography. The enthusiasm of Edmund Astley Prentis, fellow-
Chelseaite and fellow-alumnus of Columbia, has been very
helpful. I have had the pleasure also of the friendship of
Milton Halsey Thomas, archivist of Columbia, whose gracious kindness has been matched by his learning on all
things connected with Moore's alma mater.

I am indebted in varied and special ways to the following: The Rt. Rev. Robert H. Mize, D.D., retired Bishop of Salina, Kansas, and the Rev. Robert H. Mize, Jr.; the Rev. Cuthbert A. Simpson, D.D., Regius Professor of Hebrew and Canon of Christ Church, Oxford; the Very Rev. Hughell E. W. Fosbroke, D.D., Dean Emeritus and sometime Professor of Old Testament at the General Theological Seminary; his successor, the Very Rev. Lawrence Rose, D.D., present Dean; the Rev. Robert C. Dentan, D.D., Professor of Old Testament, and Dr. Niels H. Sonne, Librarian; the Rev. Edward R. Hardy, D.D., Professor of Church History at Berkeley Divinity School; the Rev. Henry P. Van Dusen, D.D., President, and the Rev. Samuel D. Terrien, D.D., Professor, of Union Theological Seminary; the Rev. Dr. William W. Manross of the Church Historical Society; Rabbi Louis Finkelstein, D.D., President of the Jewish Theological Seminary, and Dr. Gerson D. Cohen, Librarian; Prof. Irving Linn, of Yeshiva University; Prof. Thomas Ollive Mabbott of Hunter College; Prof. Charles W. Jones of the University of California; Miss Elizabeth E. Kent of St. Paul's Church, Troy, New York; Miss Helene Owen, parish recorder of Trinity Church, New York; Miss Edna A. Reading, secretary of St. Luke's Chapel, Trinity Parish, New York; the Rt. Rev. Joseph S. Minnis, D.D., Bishop of Colorado and former Vicar of the Chapel of the Intercession, Trinity Parish, New York; the Rev. Percy L. Urban, formerly of St. Peter's Church, Chelsea, and Miss Jean P. Miller, parish assistant; the Rev. Richard E. McEvoy, Rector, and Deaconess Lydia M. Ramsay, of St. Mark's Church-in-the-Bouwerie; the Rev. Lockett Fort Ballard, D.D., Rector, and the Rev. Robert B. Cook, Curate, Trinity Church, Newport, R. I.; Mrs. Isabelle Entrikin, U. S. Embassy, Santiago, Chile, and the late Mrs. Emmet Finley, Huntington, Long Island, authorities on Mrs. Sarah J. Hale and her Godey's Lady's

Book; and Walter Robert Johnson, musician and friend. The Rev. Prof. Robert S. Bosher of the General Theological Seminary has made available a copy of Dr. Moore's last portrait, now in the seminary refectory.

It is also a pleasure to state my obligation to librarians and their assistants at the New-York Historical Society, the Frick Art Reference Library, Long Island Historical Society, Library of Congress, the law division of the State Library, Albany, N. Y., the department of western manuscripts of the Bodleian Library, Oxford; the City Art Gallery, Bristol, England; the Colonial Secretary's Office, Bahamas; the Secretariat, Jamaica, B. W. I.; Colonial Office, London, England; the National Academy of Design, New York; American Antiquarian Society, Worcester, Mass.; New York University, Yale University, Newport Historical Society, Rhode Island Historical Society, New York Society Library, Masonic Library of New York Grand Lodge, Ossining Historical Society, the Church Club of New York, the New York Public Library, and especially its Municipal Reference Library branch, St. Nicholas Society, St. Andrew's Society, the New York Bible Society, the American Bible Society, James N. Wells' Sons, and the special collections division and Columbiana Room of Columbia University.

SAMUEL WHITE PATTERSON

Contents

Illustrations

THE POET OF CHRISTMAS EVE

'Twas the night before Christmas, when all through
      the house
Not a creature was stirring, not even a mouse;
The stockings were hung by the chimney with care,
In hopes that St. Nicholas soon would be there;
The children were nestled all snug in their beds,
While visions of sugar-plums danced in their heads;
And Mamma in her 'kerchief, and I in my cap,
Had just settled our brains for a long winter's nap;
When out on the lawn there arose such a clatter,
I sprang from the bed to see what what was the matter.
Away to the window I flew like a flash,
Tore open the shutters and threw up the sash.
The moon, on the breast of the new-fallen snow,
Gave the lustre of mid-day to objects below,
When, what to my wondering eyes should appear,
But a miniature sleigh, and eight tiny rein-deer,
With a little old driver, so lively and quick,
I knew in a moment it must be St. Nick.
More rapid than eagles his coursers they came,
And he whistled, and shouted, and called them by name;
"Now, _Dasher_! now, _Dancer_! now, _Prancer_ and _Vixen_!
On, _Comet_! on, _Cupid_! on, _Donder_ and _Blitzen_!
To the top of the porch! to the top of the wall!
Now dash away! dash away! dash away all!"

FACSIMILE OF CLEMENT CLARKE MOORE'S HANDWRITTEN COPY OF
"A VISIT FROM ST. NICHOLAS"

As dry leaves that before the wild hurricane fly,
When they meet with an obstacle, mount to the sky;
So up to the house-top the coursers they flew,
With the sleigh full of Toys, and St. Nicholas too.
And then, in a twinkling, I heard on the roof
The prancing and pawing of each little hoof —
As I drew in my head, and was turning around,
Down the chimney St. Nicholas came with a bound.
He was dressed all in fur, from his head to his foot,
And his clothes were all tarnished with ashes and soot;
A bundle of Toys he had flung on his back,
And he look'd like a pedlar just opening his pack.
His eyes — how they twinkled! His dimples how merry!
His cheeks were like roses, his nose like a cherry!
His droll little mouth was drawn up like a bow,
And the beard of his chin was as white as the snow;
The stump of a pipe he held tight in his teeth,
And the smoke it encircled his head like a wreath;
He had a broad face and a little round belly
That shook, when he laughed, like a bowl full of jelly.
He was chubby and plump, a right jolly old elf,
And I laughed, when I saw him, in spite of myself;
A wink of his eye and a twist of his head,
Soon gave me to know I had nothing to dread;

He spoke not a word, but went straight to his work,
And fill'd all the stockings; then turned with a jerk,
And laying his finger aside of his nose,
And giving a nod, up the chimney he rose;
He sprang to his sleigh, to his team gave a whistle,
And away they all flew like the down of a thistle.
But I heard him exclaim, ere he drove out of sight,
"Happy Christmas to all, and to all a good night."

Clement C. Moore,
1862, March 13th originally written
many years ago.

CHAPTER ONE

" 'T was the Night Before Christmas "

EVER since St. Nicholas festivities became part of Christmas Eve, the children at Chelsea House had enjoyed themselves to the full, year after year. Chelsea House stood on a cliff or bluff, which extended along the west side of Manhattan Island above the Hudson River, a few miles north of New York City. We are not interested in every Christmas Eve—in just one: in the year 1822. Clement C. Moore, who lived in Chelsea House, was a scholar of note and taught Greek and oriental languages at the theological seminary near his home. But he was not a professor this evening. He was simply a loving and thoughtful father to his six children. Hebrew verbs and nouns were forgotten. For his interest was in boys and girls, his own sons and daughters particularly: Margaret, Charity, Benjamin, Mary, Clement, and Emily. How could he make them happy? Then, too, there was Mother—his dear Eliza; and there was Grandma Moore, as sprightly as anyone in the household.

Sometime in the afternoon of the day before Christmas, Clement Clarke Moore—to give him his full name—called for his sleigh and his horses. He put on his warmest clothes, not forgetting his big fur cap and high top boots. Dearest Eliza took care of all of these, with Margaret, the oldest girl, now seven, doing her best to help, and Grandma graciously supervising everything. Father was about to go to Washington Market at Fulton and Vesey Streets, two short blocks west of St. Paul's Church. He had attended historic St. Paul's as a boy.

The day was a typical December day in New York—cold and a bit dreary. Snow had been falling all night, piling up great banks of heavy, wet flakes as far as eye could see from the windows of Chelsea House. Doubtless, Peter, the handyman, had had a slave clear a narrow cut through the snow from door to sleigh-step.

It is quite possible that Patrick, the coachman, went along. He may have been holding the reins as Father Moore stepped to his seat. A nod to go, and the horses' hooves struck hard to gain a surer footing as they took the shorter southeast path out of the grounds. They were presently beyond the gate to Ninth Avenue, a new north-south road. There was no paving as yet—only a rough, country road—for, only a short while before, walnut and apple trees grew where the sleigh now slid smoothly along.

Christmas without a turkey would be no Christmas at all except of course for religious services in the morning. The red-brick tower of St. Luke's-in-the-Fields, where the Moore family worshipped, could be faintly seen far down on Hudson Street. Clement Moore had helped found the church and had supervised the building of the modest edifice with all its unassuming dignity, reflective of his own.

The trip to the market was not easy. Snow was everywhere, with rarely a clear spot.

At last, Father Moore handed the reins to his coachman, Patrick, and eased himself into the market; it was difficult to make headway through the deep drifts. We can see his slim figure, erect but seeming taller than he was and stouter in his heavy winter coat. He probably looked about though he knew he must have a turkey. Americans were partial to the bird. Hadn't Benjamin Franklin favored it? Hadn't he argued and argued to have it made the national bird, rather than the eagle? But how big should it be on this Christmas Eve? Well, there were one, two, three, four, five, six children; all but Emily, just eight months old, had good appetites. Margaret, seven, Charity, six, Benjamin, four, Mary, three, and Clement, two, were big enough to enjoy a slice small or large. Then there were Mother and Grandmother, and Father, of course. The kindly Moores in the kindliest of seasons would also share the festivity with their servants and slaves. So, with everyone counted, it would have to be a big bird.

At last, the big bird was selected and ready to be taken out to the sleigh. With Patrick at the reins Father Moore was free to think of the surprise he had been planning. He probably ignored the rough, uneven streets, and did not hear the hard-crunching snow under the horses' feet. But it must have been hard going now and then. There were no city lights for most of the route. As the Chelsea sleigh made its way up north past St. Luke's, Father Moore could see scarcely a house between the market and the church, save a tavern at Spring Street. Dwellings were few and far between, only twinkling lights now and again across the snow.

It would seem that as he rode on and on, the sure footsense of his horses almost alone his guide, he lilted some of the lines of "A Visit from St. Nicholas." He must have improvised again and again, even as Bobby Burns did while ploughing his Scottish fields a quarter of a century or so before.

Father Moore's ear had been musical since childhood, his mother wrote her sister, Lady Affleck, who lived in London. As with the late A. E. Housman, English poet, the experience of poetic composition was aflowing into his mind, at times all but unconsciously, at times with a sudden rush of emotion: a word, a line, perhaps a stanza.

Nothing could have been better attuned to the spirit of Christmas Eve than his treatment of St. Nicholas, ancient Bishop of Myra. He jollily transformed the man of God into the gay St. Nick, merry as Margaret, Charity, Benjamin, Mary, Clement, and Emily of Chelsea House. Far from Myra of old, St. Nicholas had traveled swiftly across the centuries but never so interestingly as within these few hours over and through fresh drifts of snow; up, up, up to the very rooftops he must go, pausing only a moment to adjust his heavy pack and poise himself on the chimney edge before going down to the hearth and to the very heart of childhood. And the first chimney on this particular Christmas Eve would be one of the several on Chelsea House.

The muse of poetry is apt to be active under such circumstances as Clement C. Moore knew on this wintry afternoon in 1822. Before he reached the gate of his broad acres he had very likely composed his twenty-eight couplets and memorized them, not too perfectly, perhaps. A change or two would be made during the recital. The artist in Moore had probably selected and arranged his material almost as it appears in the finished poem. It was to be most informal and spontaneous. No candles had burned into the night while a racked brain struggled for the right word to rhyme. For rhymed couplets they had to be. Moore's favorite versifiers linked their lines, two and two together. He was an old-fashioned poet, an imitator to a degree, but always himself.

And it would be an old-fashioned family for this old-fashioned poet to entertain with his merry verses. It was a happy family. Children were never in the way, nor allowed to get in the way. A golden glow spread round the fireside; no pampering, no self-wills running wild in "self-expres-

4

sion." Discipline the six children knew, and stern enough at times.

But this was Christmas Eve. Every one was on his best behavior. Thomas and Charles, slaves, had brought in the logs for the large fireplace, and Ann or Hester, slaves, had prepared the kitchen for the turkey. Affectionate consideration did not excuse neglected duty—the duty that lay before each member of the household from Grandmother Moore and Mother Eliza to littlest Emily; from Father Moore himself to Thomas and the colored lad Richard. The aroma of filial and parental responsibility filled the Chelsea air while the personality of the head of the household gave an elevated tone to gracious living.

On this Christmas Eve so long ago expectancy rose a-tiptoe. A bright fire blazed on the hearth in the living room which was sheltered within a house that stood foursquare to all the winds that blew. The windows, solidly set, were secure before the days of weather stripping. An oversized mirror reflected the green carpet as well as the snow outside. Water colors hung in the refined taste of the period: pictures of soldiers and of Grandfather Moore. Green wallpaper set them off to advantage and heavy gold frames lent the distinction the subjects deserved. Two tall bookcases, glass-fronted and locked, guarded ponderous volumes from frivolous handling. St. Nicholas himself, brooding compassionately over the human race, must have turned a friendly eye on this earnest but cheerful group in Chelsea House on Christmas Eve four generations past.

Let us take an imaginative look. Let us peer into the window of Chelsea House on the Eve of the Nativity in the year 1822. We have come up the darkening path near the Ninth Avenue end of what is now Twenty-second Street. Tree and bush and ground are whitened with new-fallen flakes. The gatepost light flickers uncertainly in the late

Mary Moore Ogden drawing, courtesy of the New-York Historical Society
OLD CHELSEA MANSION HOUSE

December dusk. The house looms high through the gray winter sky as twilight creeps across the coppiced landscape. It stands three stories above a low basement, wooden stoops in front and on one side, several steps leading to plain and simple doorways. A rounded canopy on four tall pillars overhangs the main portal; a straighter covering rests on six slender posts over the side entrance. A tree rises tall and leans toward the house; alongside towers a giant walnut, perfectly erect. Some distance from the front doorway grows a tree lovely in its symmetry, with balanced branches, leafless as the others are on this cold December day.

We are ready for the sleigh bells, at first far, far away, then nearer, nearer, nearer. Dusk is now semi-darkness. Only a light in a window far off illumines the sloping, snowy landscape. Lamplighters were not yet hurrying through the streets at nightfall; for Chelsea was still outside the "corporation" limits, and would be for many years.

Father will soon be mounting the side steps, stamping his feet to clear off the heavy, sticky clods of snow. Patrick will take the sleigh to the barn; a servant will bring the turkey in. The fire on the living room hearth is given a vigorous special poke by Grandma Moore, alert and sparkling at seventy-five. As Father enters, Thomas or Charles helps him off with his coat and neckerchief; a few flakes still cling to his shoulders and hat but are soon brushed aside. Every one wishes to greet him at once. All want to hear of his trip to the market. With his inimitable smile, Father looks round, saying little, waiting for silence. Then, to the surprise of Eliza, Grandmother, Margaret, Charity, Benjamin, Mary, Clement (and little Emily though she does not know why), the familiar voice begins:

'T was the night before Christmas, when all through the house

Not a creature was stirring, not even a mouse; . . .

7

The recital over, Emily is packed off to bed, with Margaret, Charity, Benjamin, Mary, and Clement not far behind. They kiss their "Good Nights" while Mother and Grandmother busy themselves at the fireplace, with Father, and Peter possibly, and a servant or two lending a hand:

The stockings were hung by the chimney with care,
In hopes that St. Nicholas soon would be there;
The children were nestled all snug in their beds,
While visions of sugar-plums danced in their heads;

Shortly, candles are blown out, the wicks pinched; the slaves bank the fires. Then:

And Mamma in her 'kerchief, and I in my cap,
Had just settled our brains for a long winter's nap;
When out on the lawn there arose such a clatter,
I sprang from the bed to see what was the matter.
Away to the window I flew like a flash,
Tore open the shutters and threw up the sash.
The moon, on the breast of the new-fallen snow,
Gave the lustre of mid-day to objects below,
When, what to my wondering eyes should appear,
But a miniature sleigh, and eight tiny rein-deer,
With a little old driver, so lively and quick,
I knew in a moment it must be St. Nick.
More rapid than eagles his coursers they came,
And he whistled, and shouted, and called them by name;
"Now, *Dasher!* now, *Dancer!* now, *Prancer* and *Vixen!*
On, *Comet!* on, *Cupid!* on, *Donder* and *Blitzen!*
To the top of the porch! to the top of the wall!
Now, dash away! dash away! dash away all!"
As dry leaves that before the wild hurricane fly,
When they meet with an obstacle, mount to the sky;
So up to the house-top the coursers they flew,
With the sleigh full of Toys, and St. Nicholas too.

8

And then, in a twinkling, I heard on the roof
The prancing and pawing of each little hoof—
As I drew in my head, and was turning around,
Down the chimney St. Nicholas came with a bound.
He was dressed all in fur, from his head to his foot,
And his clothes were all tarnished with ashes and soot;
A bundle of Toys he had flung on his back,
And he look'd like a pedlar just opening his pack.
His eyes—how they twinkled! his dimples how merry!
His cheeks were like roses, his nose like a cherry!
His droll little mouth was drawn up like a bow,
And the beard of his chin was as white as the snow;
The stump of a pipe he held tight in his teeth,
And the smoke it encircled his head like a wreath;
He had a broad face and a little round belly
That shook, when he laughed, like a bowl full of jelly.
He was chubby and plump, a right jolly old elf,
And I laughed, when I saw him, in spite of myself;
A wink of his eye and a twist of his head,
Soon gave me to know I had nothing to dread;
He spoke not a word, but went straight to his work,
And fill'd all the stockings; then turned with a jerk,
And laying his finger aside of his nose,
And giving a nod, up the chimney he rose;
He sprang to his sleigh, to his team gave a whistle,
And away they all flew like the down of a thistle.
But I heard him exclaim, ere he drove out of sight,
"Happy Christmas to all, and to all a good night."

We have entered the very heart of Never-Never-Land
under the gentle guidance of the Poet of Christmas Eve.

There is no need to be scientific—to analyze the children's
appreciation. It may be that Margaret, at seven, appeared
a little skeptical; that Charity, at six, was on the verge of
doubt, but tried hard to repel her suspicions; that Benjamin,

9

four, was the only "true believer"; that Mary, a year younger, was aware of a reality beyond her mental grasp; and that Clement, two, was somewhat fearful of St. Nick. We leave such surmising to the present-day researcher in childhood psychology. Of two things we may be certain—all five enjoyed the recital, and Father and Mother and Grandmother, too, gave not a fleeting thought to any gradation in understanding or appraisal. Nor was Father Moore thinking in his recital about the human mystery of St. Nick as a preliminary lesson on the Divine mystery of God. It was all too simple for that. The Moore children got their religion direct in a manifestly religious family.

To have created such a fantasy, to have given it verve enough for rebirth year after year for over a century and a quarter, to have inspired countless boys and girls with fresh interest in life at its sweetest and best was no mean achievement. Nor is all this one whit less because Clement Moore himself was tardy in recognizing its merit. Whether he ever fully appreciated his unique contribution to American folklore may be questioned.

The accounts of the memorable Christmas Eve of 1822 in Chelsea House are many. Now and then they seem a bit confused, but tradition based on a good deal of fact makes us reasonably sure of the picture just given. The grain of truth, at least, runs through it. We know rather much about Christmas observances in the early 1820's in homes like Clement Moore's. We know a good deal about the celebrations of December 6, St. Nicholas Day, which had enlivened many a fireside in the long years past. Now, they were generally merged but with no diminution of joy and gladness. We know a great deal about the Moores and the modest house in which they lived. The poet left us a long record of thermometer readings as he peered out of his window day after day during winters unnumbered. The setting for the visit from St. Nicholas was perfect. Above everything else, we know of the love that knitted this congenial family together and the happiness they all had in each other's company. Death had not knocked since Grandfather Moore closed his eyes five years after a stroke had laid him helpless amidst his books in "The Pulpit," his small, odd-shaped study a little to the southeast of Chelsea House.

We are in no doubt at all as to the model that Clement Moore took for St. Nick. The poet revealed his identity to an intimate friend who had asked him for a copy of the famous verses. The original St. Nick—now called Santa Claus by common consent, but not by Moore—was "a portly, rubicund Dutchman living in the neighborhood of . . . Chelsea." This unknown workman unwittingly suggested an ideal hero. How we should like to know his name! And where he came from! What happened to him in after years? What, in a word, was he really like—this "portly, rubicund Dutchman"? Did the poet add a few pounds to his weight? Was he a tiller of Chelsea soil or just a good neighbor? Did he ever trim the poet's lovely old trees, or mend his fences? Did he ever even so much as glimpse what the kindly spoken gentleman he used to meet was to make of him? At all events, anonymity has not saved this "portly, rubicund Dutchman" from never-ending fame.

"A Visit from St. Nicholas" was not a literary Topsy who grew without a family or ancestral background. The *Spectator*, a New York paper, had published an interesting piece of verse on December 1, 1815:

Oh good holy man! Whom we Sancte Claus name,
The Nursery your praise shall proclaim:
The day of your joyful visit returns,
When each little bosom with gratitude burns,
For the gifts which at night you so kindly impart
For the girls of your love, and the boys of your heart.

Oh! Come with your paniers and pockets well stow'd,
Our stockings shall help you to lighten your load,
As close to the fireside gaily they swing,
While delighted we dream of the presents you bring.

Oh! Bring the bright Orange so juicy and sweet,
Bring almonds and raisins to heighten the treat;
Rich waffles and dough-nuts must not be forgot,
Nor Crullers and Oley-Cooks fresh from the pot.
But of all these fine presents your Saintship can find,
Oh! leave not the famous big Cookies behind
Or if in your hurry one thing you mislay,
Let that be the Rod—and oh! keep it away.

Then holy St. Nicholas! all the year,
Our books we will love and our parents revere,
From naughty behavior we'll always refrain,
In hopes that you'll come and reward us again.

Other lines, too, must have been ringing in Clement Moore's ears for a long time before his trip to Washington Market and his recital at Chelsea's fireside. They were published by a former neighbor, William B. Gilley, at his shop on lower Broadway not very far from where the Moores once lived in wintertime. "The Children's Friend" appeared anonymously in 1821, only a year before the historic evening at Chelsea House:

Old Santeclaus with much delight
His reindeer drives this frosty night,
O'er chimney tops, and tracks of snow,
To bring his yearly gifts to you.
The steady friend of virtuous youth,
The friend of duty, and of truth,
Each Christmas eve he joys to come
Where love and peace have made their home.

12

1

Old Santeclaus with much delight
His reindeer drives this frosty night,
O'er chimney tops, and tracks of snow,
To bring his yearly gifts to you.

Through many houses he has been,
And various beds and stockings seen;
Some, white as snow, and neatly mended,
Others, that seem'd for pigs intended.

Where e'er I found good girls and boys,
That hated quarrels, strife and noise,
I left an apple, or a tart,
Or wooden gun, or painted cart;

To some I gave a pretty doll,
To some a peg-top, or a ball;
No crackers, cannons, squibs, or rockets,
To blow their eyes up, or their pockets.

No drums to stun their mother's ear,
Nor swords to make their sisters fear,
But pretty books to store their mind
With knowledge of each various kind.

But where I found the children naughty,
In manners rude, in temper haughty,
Thankless to parents, liars, swearers,
Boxers, or cheats, or base tale-bearers,
I left a long, black birchen rod,
Such as the dread command of God
Directs a Parent's hand to use
When virtue's path his sons refuse.

It will be noted that Moore took the meter from the *Spectator* verses—anapests, they are called—but much of his imagery is from "The Children's Friend." It should be noted, however, that neither of these earlier poems would have endeared itself to the world of childhood as has "A Visit from St. Nicholas." Clement C. Moore's contribution was the spark that gave them life—lasting life. It is very like what Shakespeare did with the plots he found in Plutarch's

Lives. Shakespeare's *Julius Caesar,* for instance, is both like and unlike Plutarch's, even as Clement C. Moore's St. Nick in "A Visit from St. Nicholas" is like and unlike Santa Claus in "The Children's Friend." Art transformed each and made it live.

Moore's long-term indebtedness is apparent as we study the St. Nicholas legends of other times. Some believe that the cult of the saintly Bishop of Myra was not in great vogue in Dutch colonial days, but the scholarly Clement Moore was familiar with much that his critics may not have known. It is true that saints, bishops, and other holy men not mentioned in the Bible were not in the best standing; nevertheless there is no denying the fact that the story of St. Nicholas had an irresistible appeal to the popular imagination: his compassion, his self-giving, his love of the lowly and indeed of all mankind. On his day in December, folks had long made merry as we see in the *Spectator* verses quoted above; but this had become the exception, Christmas Eve taking over from December 6. Nor should we ignore the fact that Eliza Moore, the poet's wife, was of Dutch ancestry on her mother's side.

The St. Nicholas cult, if so it may be called, was revived after the War for Independence and prepared the way for Washington Irving's celebrated book, *The Knickerbocker's History of New York,* which was published only a few years before "A Visit from St. Nicholas" was recited at Chelsea House. Oloffe Van Kortlandt captured the inward eye of Clement C. Moore as he did many another. There were tongues that wagged in disapproval of such a travesty upon Dutch ancestors; important and influential tongues they often were. Even Moore's good friend, Gulian C. Verplanck, shook his learned head at Dietrich Knickerbocker, who everybody understood was Washington Irving, brother of Moore's classmate, Peter Irving, at Columbia College.

Now, "the sage Oloffe lived in the castle at Communipaw," that is, Hoboken, across the Hudson in plain sight of Chelsea House windows. Oloffe "dreamed a dream—and lo, the good St. Nicholas came riding over the tops of the trees, in that self-same wagon wherein he brings his yearly presents to children." As he descended the chimney, he "lit his pipe by the fire, and sat himself down and smoked; the smoke from his pipe ascended into the air and spread like a cloud overhead. And Oloffe bethought him, and he hastened and climbed to the top of the tallest trees, and saw the smoke spread over a great extent of the country. . . . And when St. Nicholas had smoked his pipe, he twisted it in his hatband, and laying his finger beside his nose, gave the astonished Van Kortlandt a very significant look; then, mounting his wagon, he returned over the tree-tops and disappeared. . . . And the people lifted up their voices and blessed the good St. Nicholas. . . . "

There can be little doubt that Moore had read these words. It may be that he had read them to his older children, Margaret, Charity, and Benjamin; or Eliza had. Surely, Irving's *Knickerbocker's History* was one of the less weighty books kept outside the two tall, glass-doored cases.

The poet's alchemy made verse of prose. The wagon became a sleigh, the single reindeer of "The Children's Friend" grew to eight. Some say that Moore had been reading Michael Drayton's poetry, of which he was fond, we know. Drayton's *Nimphidia*, a fairyland epic, gives Queen Mab twelve maids who very possibly suggested Moore's names for St. Nick's "eight tiny reindeer": *Dasher* and *Dancer*, *Prancer* and *Vixen*, *Comet* and *Cupid*, *Donder* and *Blitzen*.

However, Clement Moore was not a mere adapter, or imitator. He was original as Shakespeare though not, to be sure, on so large a scale. Even if the necessity of rhyme prompted it, St. Nick, as all the world knows him, was his creation. But, of course, Santa Claus and St. Nick had been familiar to New York ever since James Rivington's *Gazetteer* of December 23, 1773. This New York printer, whom Moore knew, told his readers that the anniversary of St. Nicholas, or Santa Claus, had been gaily celebrated on the Monday of a fortnight or so ago.

John Pintard, distinguished New Yorker of our early national period, had also popularized the Bishop of Myra in his famous *Almanac*. He listed the saint's day with Christmas Day, New Year's Day, Independence Day, and others. Here were secular and religious days intermingled in a fashion to shock Chelsea's churchly good breeding. Strict Anglican upbringing, such as the Moores', would not countenance so unholy a mixture of sacred and profane.

It was farthest from Clement Moore's thought to entertain posterity. He was reciting his verses for Margaret, Charity, Benjamin, Mary, Clement; and for little Emily, too, as she sat gleeful on Mother's knee, saw the rapt faces, and heard the happy laughs of brothers and sisters. The poet left no doubt as to his purpose. He composed the verses simply and solely for his own children, as a sort of Christmas present.

The story of what happened to "A Visit from St. Nicholas" after Christmas Eve is a fairly familiar one. The poet tells us that some time later, not very long apparently, the verses "were copied by a relative . . . in her album." Who she was he does not say. She let a friend from Troy copy them and we are pretty sure that this friend was Miss Harriet Butler, daughter of the Rev. David Butler of St. Paul's Church, Troy, New York. Her brother was the Rev. Clement Butler, named after the poet of Chelsea. The families were good friends; they may even have been distantly related, but their ties were more probably of mind and spirit than of blood. Clement Moore's father, Bishop Benjamin Moore, had jour-

17

neyed to Troy to institute, that is, install, Harriet's father as rector of St. Paul's. They were all of the so-called Connecticut school of religious thought, sometimes referred to as the Seabury School. Samuel Seabury, the first Bishop of the Episcopal Church, was head of the diocese of Connecticut.

Miss Butler took Moore's jolly couplets to Editor Orville L. Holley of the Troy *Sentinel,* who very likely knew the Moores or at least had met Bishop Moore. Troy was a small town; every one knew every one else, and all the visitors besides. As editor of the *Sentinel* Mr. Holley would certainly learn of any one who came to see the rector of St. Paul's. In his issue of December 23, 1823, Holley published "An Account of a Visit from St. Nicholas." Thus the poem got its name. "We do not know," wrote Mr. Holley, "to whom we are indebted for the following description of that unwearied patron of music—that homely and delightful personage of parental kindness—Santa Claus—his costume, and his equipage, as he goes about visiting the firesides of this happy land, laden with Christmas bounties. There is . . . a spirit of cordial goodness in it, a playfulness of fancy, and a benevolent alacrity to enter into the feelings and promote the simple pleasures of children, which are altogether charming."

Editor Holley was basking in the atmosphere of President Monroe's "era of good feeling," as he wrote of "this happy land" of ours. He expressed his cordial thanks to whoever had sent him these Christmas verses. He hoped that his "little patrons, both lads and lassies," would accept the poem "as a proof of our unfeigned goodwill towards them—as a token of our warmest wish that they may have many a merry Christmas; that they may long retain their beautiful relics of homebred joys, which derive their flavor from filial piety and fraternal love, and which they may be assured are the least alloyed that time can furnish them; and that they may never part with that simplicity of character, which is their fairest ornament, and for the sake of which they have been pronounced, by Authority which none can gainsay, the types of such of us as shall inherit the kingdom of heaven."

Much ado has been made of Mr. Holley's unawareness of the identity of the person who gave him the copy of "A Visit from St. Nicholas." Much more has been said about his ignorance of the author. It need not trouble us in either case. As a matter of fact—or better, of reasonable guess— Mr. Holley had a strong notion as to who the fair young person was, and he may have surmised the poet's name. He omitted the lady's name, we may be sure, because it was not nice for girls in his day to break into print. Miss Butler, as the daughter of a clergyman, might have been embarrassed; surely, her reverend father would have been. As a leading newspaper man, Holley must have heard of the name of Clement Clarke Moore, professor in the newly established General Theological Seminary in New York. But he held his peace, and the Moores shunned publicity as they would the plague.

The New York *Morning Courier* printed "A Visit from St. Nicholas" on January 1, 1829, and the Troy *Sentinel* again the same year, when Editor Holley ventured to unveil the poet's identity behind some full-guarded words. The author, he observed, was "a gentleman of more merit as a scholar and writer than many of more noisy pretensions." It is not hard to see how Mr. Holley was trying to protect the professor of oriental languages from unseemly curiosity.

The Schenectady *Whig* published the verses at Christmastime 1832. Upstate New York newspapers, generally, found them favored by old as well as young. At various times and places, "A Visit from St. Nicholas" became a "carrier's address" or flash advertisement, a device to help newsboys at-

A Myron King woodcut of St. Nick from the Troy "Sentinel"

ILLUSTRATION FROM "ACCOUNT OF A VISIT FROM ST. NICHOLAS, OR SANTA CLAUS," AS PRINTED BY N. TUTTLE

tract customers as they shouted "Extra," or more often "Wuxtry," on street corners. Horace Greeley encouraged carriers' addresses to promote his New York *Daily Tribune* sales.

The first illustrated edition of "A Visit," still anonymous, was Myron King's in the early 1830's. King was a Troy engraver with a sure instinct for glamor within the bounds of good taste. He depicted Santa Claus, as St. Nick was very early called, without a model to go by other than the poet's, and yet the jolly old elf comes alive, is very real. King's "eight tiny reindeer" seem drawn from life. Unknowingly, this obscure engraver had set Clement Moore's Christmas hero on the highroad to poetry's hall of fame. Though successors of his creation have appeared in unnumbered illustrated editions of the Chelsea jingle, the initial inspiration should be accredited to Myron King of Troy, after Clement C. Moore himself.

Christmastide was observed at Chelsea House for years after 1822. A decade later, Grandmother Moore wrote her sister in London: "Here is another Xmas coming, children all expectation and their dear father preparing little presents to make them happy. . . . " But there does not appear to have been another like the Christmas Eve when Margaret, Charity, Benjamin, Mary, Clement, and Emily first heard their "dear father" introduce St. Nicholas at Chelsea House.

CHAPTER TWO

The Poet's Goodly Heritage in Old and New Chelsea

O N BOTH sides of his house, Clement Clarke Moore, Poet of Chelsea and Poet of Christmas Eve, was mainly of English stock. French, Scottish, and Irish strains were also traceable. The earls of Mt. Cashell and Drogheda were among his forebears. The family settled very early in Kent in southeast England. The name had variants: Moore, More, Moor, Meor, and Mure, with Moore the most frequent, especially as the centuries passed. Some have seen a suggestion of French or Moorish in Moor, but it is doubtful.

The first of the name, the first of importance, that is, seems to have been Thomas de la More, who crossed the English Channel in the fall of 1066 to fight at Hastings and help William of Normandy to the throne of England. Better than five hundred years later, in September 1609, John Moor entered New York harbor with Henry Hudson aboard the *Half-Moon.*

The Rev. John Moore, an Independent clergyman, was Clement C. Moore's first American ancestor to settle here. He crossed the Atlantic in the first years of the seventeenth century, and journeyed to Lynn, Massachusetts, where he became a civic leader, interesting himself in the union of the New England colonies as well as in the financial af-

fairs of Harvard College. In 1647, he removed to South-
ampton, Long Island, then to Middleburg, afterward called
Newtown and now Elmhurst. His friendly dealings with the
Indians met with considerable success at Newtown. An Indian deed exists for forty acres; it is dated April 12, 1656.
Newtown folk were so well pleased with his efforts that they
voted him title to a town house and thirty acres. Many
years after his death they conveyed eighty acres to his
children in recognition of his services to the community and
to the country roundabout. Of greater popular interest is
the Moore variety of apples. Newtown pippins became famous, and they are to this day.

Captain Samuel Moore, the clergyman's son, built the
house in which Benjamin and William Moore, Clement's
father and uncle respectively, were born in the mid-eighteenth century. They were sons of another Samuel who occupied the original Moore homestead that was replaced
in 1776 by a small farmhouse, which stood until recently,
with a tall, wide-spreading well sweep conspicuous in the
front yard. The house was torn down a few years ago to
make way for the Elmhurst subway station, but the old barn
continued to stand until swift-moving changes swept it, too,
away.

The old Moore building had had its historic moments.
Sir William Howe, British commander, made it his headquarters for a time during the Revolution. England's Duke
of Clarence, later King William IV, was a guest there. Clement Moore's mother remembered being introduced to him
in New York. Today, the only reminder of the house and of
the once sizeable estate is a triangular park, a breathing
place for a crowded neighborhood, on Broadway, Elmhurst.
A sign atop an iron upright tells the passerby that on this
spot stood the "Ancestral home of Dr. C. C. Moore, author
of 'T was the Night Before Christmas."

Children from nearby churches used to sing carols at the homestead door and members of the Moore family bade them "A Merry Christmas." For some reason Clement Moore's "Happy Christmas" at the close of his famous poem did not register with future generations although "Happy New Year" and "Happy Birthday" did. All folklore has its inconsistencies. More important is it that Moore's St. Nick became part of America's homespun inheritance.

Whether the Newtown festivities inspired the Poet of Christmas Eve is an open question. It is not improbable. Lingering memories of earlier days often help frame patterns of adult fancy. However, that he composed "A Visit from St. Nicholas" at Newtown, is not to be thought of seriously. The tradition in Chelsea on Manhattan Island, where Moore spent most of his life, rules out the old farmhouse's chimneys as the first that good St. Nick descended on his historic visit at Christmastime 1822.

The Moores were a prolific family. Generally speaking they were also independent, as the Rev. John Moore was religiously. They followed their own bent occupationally, though for a time keeping very close to the soil. They were usually in easy circumstances, and they saw to it that marital alliances did not lessen the easiness. They were connected with the wealthy and justly influential Bayards, Pintards, and Livingstons. Through the years we find them spreading across the East River to New York, up the Hudson and farther upstate, to New Jersey and Pennsylvania; and beyond, to Virginia and points south. Some of them trekked to Long Island Sound and took sail for Connecticut.

Benjamin Moore, father of the poet, entered King's College at sixteen. He had several college mates who made their mark: Gouverneur Morris, conspicuously, as a member of the Continental Congress and of the Constitutional Convention of 1787. Since King's College was a day school it is not a mere guess that the youthful Benjamin boarded in the city, going home weekends. If King's had had a theological course he would most likely have taken it.

Set as the College was in strongly English surroundings, circumstances as well as location gave it an atmosphere which the Established Church services helped create and enrich. Chapel prayers reminded one of Trinity Church which had given the school its site, first on Rector Street and then on what is now Park Place. But King's College, strictly speaking, was not a Church institution of higher learning. For there were alert and powerful religious forces in the city which had not taken kindly to its founding. Indeed, they stoutly opposed the establishment of any institution Anglican-controlled. Through its opposition, the Whig Club, in particular, whose leaders were largely Yale men, helped make the College virtually non-sectarian and less exclusive —certainly for the mid-eighteenth century. The politic Dr. Samuel Johnson, an Anglican clergyman who served as first president of King's, tactfully observed: "And that the people may be the better satisfied in sending their children for education to this college, there is no intention to impose on the scholars the peculiar tenets of any particular sect of Christians. . . . "

So far as the course of study was concerned, there was general agreement on all sides. The liberal arts gave the only education that most citizens thought worth while. Girls, of course, were far from the academic scene, presumably content with household chores until afforded an opportunity to continue the chores in their own homes the rest of their lives.

Benjamin Moore was thus a student in one of the very few colleges of his day; and it was equal to the best at Cambridge, Williamsburg, New Haven, and Princeton. He was well grounded in the classics and thoroughly trained to think with the logic of mathematical science. His home and church imbued him with a religious seriousness which turned his attention to the ministerial calling. Since the College did not help him much in this regard he was practically self-taught under the guidance of the Reverend John Ogilvie of Trinity. Young Moore might have gone abroad, to Cambridge perhaps, as other like-minded youths often did. His family, while not wealthy, had the money to send him, with possible aid from the church.

After six years of post-college effort, Benjamin Moore journeyed to England in 1774 for ordination. As yet, there was no American episcopate. Within a few months, he was ordered deacon and ordained presbyter, or priest. This was not the common practice in the Church of England, but it was common enough when candidates came from the distant Colonies and could not stay too long abroad. In Moore's favor, also, was his plan to serve as soon as possible on the Trinity staff. The times were uncertain; delays might mean remaining in England indefinitely. Nobody could be sure what the next hour would bring forth. In September, there were rumors of a Continental Congress in Philadelphia. The youthful cleric was a staunch subject of his King, loyal as Trinity Church itself.

Not long after the Rev. Benjamin Moore landed in America he heard of the first great step taken by the Colonies and wondered, as many another did: Whither his native land? Whither his own feet, shod with the Gospel of Peace? He had taken an oath of allegiance to the Crown or he never could have kneeled before the Bishop of London for the laying on of hands. In May 1775 the Second Continental Congress convened in Philadelphia. Lexington and Concord had charged the political air in the City of Brotherly Love with high voltage. Events were quickening the American pulse to open revolt and, possibly, war. Indeed, Colonel

From print in William S. Perry's "The Episcopate in America"

BISHOP BENJAMIN MOORE

George Washington was soon riding to Cambridge to take command of a new army, a Continental or national army, to fight His Gracious Majesty King George III.

In less than a twelvemonth Sir William Howe evacuated Boston and removed his British regulars to New York. Not long afterward he was making his headquarters at Newtown. The boom of cannon could be heard all the way from Brooklyn Heights. Early autumn skies saw flames burst forth above New York. The Rev. Benjamin Moore found his beloved church a charred ruin. The congregation was transferred to St. Paul's, a few blocks to the north on Broadway, where he continued to minister to the flock.

To make matters worse, the rector of Trinity was a Loyalist of Loyalists, with forthright views forthrightly uttered. The Rev. Charles Inglis had served a year as acting president of King's College and was highly esteemed in British civilian and military quarters. He had split his Dover, Delaware, parish wide open, and he might do it again in New York. The moderates were concerned; they, and the peace-at-any-price men of the time, had noted a certain sweet reasonableness in Dr. Inglis's two assistants, the Rev. Samuel Provoost, out-and-out for the Americans, and the Rev. Benjamin Moore, lukewarm, still groping for the final answer. In after years Dr. Inglis became Bishop of Nova Scotia and his two Trinity assistants Bishops of New York.

The Rev. Benjamin Moore solved the difficulty that Dr. Inglis faced by marking time, without offense to anybody, royalist, loyalist, or patriot. All of the Anglican clergy had to think themselves through the same dilemma. Some went to England, others to Canada, some took the American side unabashedly, without a qualm. Oath or no oath, their argument ran, circumstances had altered the whole situation. Moore straddled until events showed him the road ahead.

In 1775 the King's College governors, later called trustees, elected the Rev. Benjamin Moore acting president in Dr. Inglis's place. A youth named Alexander Hamilton did not have to repeat the little service he had rendered the Rev. President Myles Cooper. Hamilton had harangued his fellow-students until Dr. Cooper had escaped in his night clothes to a waiting man-of-war at anchor in the Hudson. He did not return, and his successor, the even-tempered Rev. Benjamin Moore, gave not the staunchest patriot any cause to worry.

The selection of an acting head was a mere gesture. The College was closed for the duration. The governors wanted a "safe man" and got one in Moore who had all the curricular, and especially the extracurricular, qualifications: among them, a native American, a Church of England clergyman, a tolerant attitude, and a closed mouth. Acting President Benjamin Moore served until 1781. He remained on the Trinity staff and for a time held the post of deputy chaplain of the royal military hospital that had taken over the College building.

Not all of the Moores were on the fence politically. Like many another colonial family they divided on the issues of the hour. Though the calm Rev. Benjamin Moore tried to keep to the middle way, his kin, near and far, were active in civil or military affairs. Captain James Moore lost his life crossing the Delaware with Washington in the cold of Christmas night 1776. Another married a member of the prominent White family of Philadelphia. His mother-in-law had been a schoolmate of Martha Washington's and was her lifelong friend. A relative by marriage was the Rev. William White, eminent churchman and brother-in-law of the merchant-patriot, Robert Morris.

Busy as the Rev. Benjamin Moore was with the many duties that wartime imposed, he found the time to visit Chelsea House, a few miles north of Trinity. There was a viva-

John Wollaston portrait, courtesy of the Moore Family

CAPTAIN THOMAS CLARKE—FOUNDER OF CHELSEA

cious daughter of a vivacious widow in the Chelsea household. Her name was Charity Clarke. She had two unmar-
ried brothers at home and two married sisters in England:
Mary, wife of Sir Gilbert Affleck, and Maria Theresa, wife
of the Viscount Barrington, a cousin of Theodosia, who
would one day be the wife of Vice President Aaron Burr.
The younger brother, Clement Clarke, had been a freshman
at King's College when Charity's suitor was a senior.

Miss Charity Clarke's father, Captain Thomas, had served
his King in the royal provincial forces during the War of the
Austrian Succession. He had married Mary Stillwell in 1745
when he was 53. Upon retiring from the army he did not go
back to England but settled in New York, where he acquired ninety-four acres of land from Jacob Somerindyk and
his wife. The property is quaintly described in the deed as
"all that farm or plantation and tract of land, situate, lying
and being in the Bassau Bowery, in the Out Ward, and on
the West side of Manhattan Island, beginning at a certain
ditch by the river side belonging to Yellis Mandeville, and
bounded on the West by the Hudson River, on the East by
land of John Horn, on the North by land of Widow Cowen-
hoven and Brandt Schuyler, and on the South by land of
Sir Peter Warren and Yellis Mandeville."

This "Bassau Bowery" or "Bouwerie"—Dutch for "farm in
the woods"—had been Governor Van Twiller's tobacco plantation and more anciently an Indian cross-island carrying-
place called *Sappokanican* in the Algonquin tongue. Here
copper-skinned men fished in small streams, hunted in
wooded spots, courted and wed, begat chiefs and war-
riors, and were content "in that state of life to which it had
pleased God to call them," as Captain Clarke's catechism
advised all Christian men to be.

The Clarke and Stillwell families had been British for
generations; Mary Stillwell's more prominent than Thomas

Clarke's. Their property in America reflected a lingering nostalgia for the old country and, in particular, for Chelsea, London. Sir Thomas More had made Chelsea famous in the sixteenth century; Thomas Carlyle would add a lustrous halo in the nineteenth, and American-born T. S. Eliot keep it alive in this twentieth century of ours. The veteran's hospital or home that Captain Clarke had seen times without number bobbed up in his memory so often that he called his new home Chelsea.

The Chelsea farm stretched north and south along the Fitzroy Road, now Eighth Avenue, from Twenty-first Street to Twenty-fourth. To the west flowed the river over muddy flats at the foot of Chelsea ridge, now Tenth Avenue. A road or, rather, wide lane, made its way across the Island from present Broadway to the Clarke acres; officially, it was the Abingdon Road but popularly, Lover's Lane, an east-west route to the center of Manhattan. Another was Monument Lane, later renamed Greenwich Avenue. Fitzroy and Abingdon recalled the titled husbands of Sir Peter Warren's daughters. At the eastern end of Abingdon Road lay the Horn farm, part of which, in years to come, Clement Moore purchased and added to his inherited estate.

A short walk to the south of Chelsea, along Fourteenth Street of today, a shallow cove or bay indented the riverfront near Washington and Twelfth Streets; northward extended a rocky, hilly section to marshes a quarter of a mile from Captain Clarke's farm. "The rippling of the water on the river's shore," we are told in an old account, was the only sound to break the quietude. Miasmal marshes sent mosquitoes and unpleasant odors southward, causing feverish illness now and then at Chelsea House.

Most of the Clarke children were born in England. Miss Charity came to America with her parents and brothers and was never able to shake off her Britishness entirely. Her son, the poet, found the year of her birth, 1747, in an old pocket-book among her belongings after her death. We cannot tell, nor even guess, which side Captain Clarke might have taken in the Revolution. He had been sympathetic with George II's campaigns in behalf of Maria Theresa, Empress of Austria, and had served in the royal forces. He called a daughter Maria Theresa; we find the name repeated among his great grandchildren. Death spared him the ultimate decision. His frame dwelling burned down before the first faint echo of war floated across his Chelsea fields. It was in mid-February 1774—the cruelest of months. When fire broke out, piercing winds tossed everything to the flames. The aging veteran—in his eighties now—suffered critically, but lingered two years at a neighboring farmhouse, where he died.

The captain left his widow well off financially; all went to her after the daughter had been given three thousand pounds. Molly Clarke was not a weeping widow, but an indomitable one. Women of her colonial type were apt to be. She set herself the task of rebuilding a new Chelsea House and had it made of brick, two stories high; the poet added a third many years later. As an elderly widow she continued to show considerable intellectual as well as physical vigor, but she did not see eye to eye with her sprightly daughter on the issues of the hour.

With her excellent mind, and the three thousand pounds from her father, Miss Charity would have been welcome in the salons of London and Paris, where intellectual women liked to display their scintillating wit. Upon her return from a visit with her cousin Joseph Jekyll of Lincoln's Inn, she corresponded with him for some time. Her thank-you note included very definite views which she had mulled over on the eleven-week voyage. And they did not accord with his by any means. With a witty sally she let him understand how

John Wollaston portrait, courtesy of the Moore Family
MARY STILLWELL CLARKE

superior her Chelsea was to his London. How much she enjoyed living under the Crown! But, remember, Cousin Joseph, if Parliament should be silly enough to make another "show of oppression," such as the Stamp Act of odious memory, Americans would exert themselves to the utmost. "Unruly mobs we leave to England, they don't govern America."

Charity's cousin was also wrong about the amusements in New York in so grave a time of crisis. There were, to be sure, she admitted, a good many parties, but with this difference: American gentlemen made no distinctions as to rank, "except to the Governor's lady." Finally, let Cousin Joseph note carefully: "My countrymen will suffer all ills . . . rather than give up one jot of their just rights."

Mother Clarke was loyal still to the homeland though she tried to hold her peace. A stray shot from a British frigate in the Hudson irritated her, but when Americans gained control of the city, Washington's Continentals were billeted at Chelsea House. Molly Clarke could keep her temper no longer. Some of the "rebel soldiers" caused "so much distress," Grandson Clement Moore tells us, "that one of the officers represented their condition" to the commander-in-chief. Precisely what "their condition" may have been is not clear, but hard liquor flowed pretty freely at times.

One day, in the sunshine of Bowling Green, a stalwart horseman mounted his big white charger at the Kennedy House, now No. 1 Broadway. He started north toward Chelsea. Galloping up Fitzroy Road to the bend at what is now Twenty-second Street, thence west by north, he reined in at the Widow Clarke's gatepost. With a gentlewoman's charm and grace she received General George Washington, rebel though he was, and escorted him to her broad fireside in the living room, which was plainly but comfortably furnished. Mistress Clarke respected her caller's dignified demeanor, but was not at all awed. Soft words alone would never do.

He must give her his assurance that her worries from petty annoyances were over. And he did. His men would mind their own business in future. The widow had no further cause for complaint.

The war dragged on. The British took New York and beyond, to Chelsea and farther north. Since the commanding officer of Hessian mercenaries stationed in Chelsea was civil, Molly Clarke tolerated the nuisance. Then came winter and bitter cold. Her fruit trees made good firewood when the Hessians, heavy-booted though they were, felt the nipping river breezes. War or no war, the widow would have none of this nonsense and vigorously protested. Thereafter, foreign soldiers must warm themselves without benefit of the trees she had planted and nursed from saplings.

At war's end the Chelsea household reconciled itself to the political *status quo*. The courts helped. They freed Trinity Church from control of the Church of England as the Treaty of Peace freed the country from the government of England. The Rev. Benjamin Moore felt absolved from his oath of allegiance. Time now to make Miss Charity Clarke his wife. She was thirty-one, he thirty. At the altar of Trinity Church piety, intellect, and modest means married intellect and plenty.

On July 15, 1779, a son was born at Chelsea House. On August 11, he was baptized Clement Clarke Moore as a "child of God and an inheritor of the kingdom of heaven." Dr. Jonathan Odell, a former surgeon in the royal army, came from St. Mary's, Burlington, to be sponsor at the Trinity font. He was a Tory to the bone and later a refugee to Canada. The Moores do not appear to have kept up his acquaintance.

Columbia's Top Man, Class of 1798

LEMENT CLARKE MOORE was one of the most fortunate
of men. He was born to culture and the means to
sustain it. He would have been happy in the Renaissance and pleased to know Cosimo the Elder, merchant and
patron of the arts in the fifteenth century, but he could never
have approved the exile of enemies to make oneself safe and
secure.

Young Moore had no need to worry about employment for
financial return. As an only child he enjoyed everything,
especially those finer things of life, which a devoted family
in a rural society willingly and generously provided. If so
minded he might have followed the way of dalliance as many
another of his generation did in the last quarter of the eighteenth century. Instead, he trod the path his parents pointed
out under the ever watchful eyes of Grandmother Clarke, a
remarkable woman in an age of remarkable women.

The family of Chelsea House gave Clement the nurture of
an ancient faith, the rudiments of a sound education. One
might expect that he would have followed his father's calling but, independent as the Moores always were, he chose
his life's work as he pleased. Of course, we do not know what
may have been discussed, perhaps warmly argued, at the in-

37

timate fireside. But Clement was in no hurry. When he made up his mind he preferred the academic gown to the priestly vestment, but the gown was always closely identified with the vestment.

Fortunate, too, was this bright and serious, yet fun-loving young man in the period in which he lived. Born in the mid-year of the Revolution he died in the mid-year of the Civil War. His life-span witnessed a social and scientific revolution as far-reaching as the political revolt that had made the Thirteen Colonies the United States of America. The first six decades of the nineteenth century—the years of Moore's mature manhood—saw expansion in various directions. The years from 1800, when he was twenty-one, to 1860, when he was eighty-one, changed the country at large as well as his own city.

Physically and culturally Clement Moore's era was a time of intellectual, social, and spiritual testing; even religion did not escape the searching eye of change. Moore did not choose to be a passive idler and spectator in the market-place. He declined to shut himself up in the ivory tower of Chelsea House on the edge of a fast-growing Manhattan Island, which would turn from rural to urban eventually, with marked effect upon the property the young man inherited.

Although the second quarter of the last century was one of tension and contention as well as of progress it was one also which interested itself in things of the mind, heart, and spirit. Moore elected to be a participant in the transformation of New York into a center of American letters and publication, which outstripped Boston and Philadelphia before his days were ended. His good friend, the versatile genius Gulian C. Verplanck, called the city "a focus of the things of the mind." He was not wholly right, but the ever-increasing presence of leaders in the higher walks of life—writers, scientists, scholars, and educators—gave point to his observation.

With all of this background of family and environment it would have been strange indeed if Clement Moore had been indifferent to the best of his time. He was blessed with a father who cared about his son's moral, spiritual, and intellectual development; he was blessed with a mother who saw to it that all the refinements of a well-balanced home were her son's to enjoy. Chelsea House was indeed a sheltered sanctuary for carefree hours.

When Clement's father had made his peace, so to speak, with the new order of affairs, after the separation from England, he followed through with sincerity and unswerving devotion. There must have been something in the air of Chelsea House to stir any keen young boy when the Rev. Benjamin Moore told the family that he was going to take part in the first inauguration of President Washington. Old Widow Clarke lived very long, with vivid memories of a sun-lit forenoon in 1789. The inaugural ceremony took place at Federal Hall, on the corner of Wall and Broad Streets. It was not far from the site of Trinity Church (which had burned years before). A family connection, General Samuel B. Webb, held the Bible on which the Chief Executive laid his hand as he took the oath of his great office, which the Hon. Robert R. Livingston, a college mate of the elder Moore's at King's, administered. Just what part the Rev. Benjamin Moore had it is not easy to say, except as a representative of the Church, and of religion generally.

Clement Moore's earliest schooling was at home under his father's wise tutelage and even wiser guidance. That young Clement learned to write the hard way—as most authors do—is amply evidenced in the following letter he sent his revered tutor in early August 1789:

CLEMENT CLARKE MOORE AS A BOY

My dear papa,

If you stay much longer we shall be tempted to come after you for we are sick of living without you. I wish you had been here last friday for there was A Balloon went up, it was very pretty little one, and it went up very prettyly Aunt Maunsel and cousin Lydia, and Aunt Watkins, are gone to the springs. I wish you would answer my letters. Are the coppers the same in Philadelphia as they are here? Jersey coppers wont pass here now. We can hardly buy anything now. I wish you would answer this letter and tell me what I ask. Fan has had fits very bad eating green apples I believe. She was very well the day before and in the morning she was very well and Betty sent her to get some chips and she brought her some, and went out with Rachel in the orchard, and Sally Rap hollowed out to her, see how fan lies under the tree, but She thought it was only some of her airs and went on, when she came home betty asked her where fan was, she said she was lying under the tree, said she, are not you ashamed to let her lye there, she came here for her health and you let her lye there such a morning as this, and she sent little Jack for her and he stayed a great while, and they sent a man to her, and he thought she was dead all frothing and foaming and he brought her home. I must tell you the rest when you come home.

C. C. Moore

Clement's mother, it seems most likely, added a postscript: "We are apprehensive Fran's fit was something of an Epilepsy. She was speechless several hours." Who Fran was, or the others the ten-year-old Clement mentions, we do not know. The balloon ascent the boy so much enjoyed was "the event" of only two days before. The New York *Packet* of August 11 printed Joseph Decker's advertisement of his exhibition "at the fort, for the benefit of the large Balloon," which would "ascend on Friday the 13th instant, at 6 o'clock in the afternoon, from a lot near the Race-ground," at Suffolk Street. This would "prevent gentlemen and boys from running the risk of breaking their necks by clambering up the Fort walls." Tickets of admission to the exhibition were priced at a shilling each. The balloon that young Clement had seen traveled nine miles northward before it alighted on the Harlem River.

The elder Moore was strict and thorough; Clement acquired a firm command of the tools of learning, which stood him in good stead to the end of his life. What the next seven years would mean in this respect may be seen in the following letter that the son wrote to his exacting mother in May 1796 when he was half way through Columbia College. He might have prepared at the Columbia Grammar School where the standards were at least as high as at the older Boston Latin School. But the Rev. Benjamin Moore had made this unnecessary. From Philadelphia young Clement wrote his "dearest Mother":

> I take my pen in hand to prepare you for being very angry with me, but, before I introduce the subject, shall endeavour to expiate, in a small degree, my fault, by giving you, according to your request, a very circumstantiall account of my conduct since my last letter, which, I think, was dated on Saturday evening. The next morning I went to Christ Church. . . . In the afternoon I heard Mr. Bissert preach in the African Church, and in the evening I enjoyed the happiness of hearing Mr. Pilmore's soft and melodious voice swelled to the highest pitch of harmony.

Young Moore goes on to tell his mother of his chat with "Peter Porcupine," William Cobbett, the greatest English newspaper man of his day. At this time he was a Tory, but in the years ahead a flaming radical in his political thinking. "In the evening I went to the theatre, but was disappointed." A visit to the mint, also; the director was not there, and only "a peep" was possible "when one of the men opened the door." The afternoon was given to Gray's gardens, which, though much neglected, seemed pleasing enough. "It would be vain to attempt mentioning all the places at which I call, dine, and drink tea. I find the Philadelphians very kind and attentive; I dine and drink tea abroad almost every day."

Then to the point of his writing "dearest Mother":

And now, with a trembling hand, I shall enter upon the subject which I dreaded so much in the beginning of my letter. This morning I went to a store of mathematical instruments. I am sure you can guess it now, and the man showed me a handsome surveying instrument upon a new construction, price 40 dollars. I had but 30 of my own, and did not know what to do, for I knew that I should not meet with such an opportunity in N. York, and it was small and neatly put up so that I could conveniently pack it in my trunk.

So, Clement borrowed ten dollars from a friend, or rather, as he put it, asked a friend to lend him the money.

Now Mama I am sure if you had been in Philadel: with me, you would not have hesitated a minute to supply the deficiency, but I am fearful that you will not be pleased with me for borrowing the money without first asking your consent; but you must consider that I had not time, if I had written, to receive an answer, and that I could not have bought one of any kind in N York. If, when I return home now, I meet your face half diffused with a smile and half contracted with a frown, I shall not only wish myself again in Philadelphia, where I meet with nothing but smiles, but I shall never forgive myself, or dare to look at you with confidence again. But, if I perceive your countenance oerspread with joy at receiving me, I shall be oerjoyed once more to see you, and fly with redoubled transports to your arms. Give my love to Papa, Grandma, Mary, and Tom. And now I am sure I have trespassed long enough on the limits of decency, in regard to the length of my letter; and shall conclude with declaring myself

Your ever affectionate Son

C C Moore

P.S. Excuse bad spelling &c, for the Post goes tomorrow morning and I have not time to be correct as it is very late.

King's College had suffered a good deal of change since Clement Moore's father attended it. With its name erased it had begun a new career as Columbia in 1784. Though an act of the state legislature had reorganized it, it remained for a time essentially the same school as in pre-Revolution days. In 1787, however, Columbia received a more liberal charter, which removed it from the state regents' control and vested authority in trustees, who, oddly enough, have never called themselves a board.

When Clement Moore went to Columbia the faculty, though not large, included able men, some with international backgrounds. Three—James Kemp, mathematics and natural philosophy; Peter Wilson, classics; and John Bisset, rhetoric and belles-lettres—were from Aberdeen, and steeped in their subjects. John McKnight, moral philosophy, was from Princeton, still under the spell of the great Scottish divine, John Witherspoon; Antoine V. Marcellin, French, was a distinguished scholar; Johann C. Kunze, Hebrew, was a Leipzig man, a very learned teacher. There was a course in chemistry and Moore took it, although his interest was primarily in the humanities. Science, however, attracted him not a little.

Professor Nathaniel Fish Moore, later Columbia's president, defined the educational ideal that dominated the college during the time of his cousin, Clement: "The old paths are those in which she ought still to walk . . . for the duties of life, and for the attainment of a blessed and glorious existence hereafter." A college, he maintained, should not merely instruct; it should educate. The student must do his work or leave, without visible tears. Society of the period placed no stigma on the non-college man, for higher education was for the few deemed fit and worthy.

Clement C. Moore graduated from Columbia at the head of his class, as his father had, thirty years earlier. His valedictory address was entitled "Gratitude." Most of his classmates became lawyers; the prestige of the legal profession had risen tremendously after the Revolution. Two of Moore's class took up medicine; only one, the ministry. Of the eighteen youths who received their diplomas at Commencement 1798 Moore alone is remembered.

The young man from Chelsea went on to his master's degree in 1801. His father had erected a queer-looking structure on Moore's Hill near Chelsea House, which he and Son Clement used as a study. The "Pulpit," as it was usually called, stood east of Ninth Avenue on Twentieth Street. Here Clement did much of his early studying; after his marriage his home became his study. The Columbia professor who seems to have directed his life's work was Dr. Johann C. Kunze, the scholar in Semitics. At all events, we find Moore busily engaged in the preparation of *A Compendious Lexicon of the Hebrew Language*. He had probably begun it shortly after graduation, if not indeed before. Since New York printers did not have Hebrew characters in their fonts, Moore had to send to Philadelphia for them. Penn's city was holding its

"The Pulpit"

From an old print

own as a publishing center, especially for scholarly books. The *Lexicon* appeared in two volumes in 1809. It was dedicated to the Rt. Rev. Benjamin Moore, D.D., "by his affectionate son."

The dedication of the *Lexicon* calls for a word of explanation. After the Revolution, when the Church of England in the Colonies was reorganized as the Protestant Episcopal Church, Dr. Provoost was elected the first Bishop of New York. He had served faithfully for a decade and a half when he felt that it was time to yield to a younger man. The Rev. Benjamin Moore was elected and in September 1801 consecrated at Trenton. Though he was to all intents and purposes the head of the diocese, which embraced the whole state of New York, he was generally regarded as an assistant to Bishop Provoost. He had followed the leisurely, scientifically minded Dr. Provoost as rector of Trinity and, it will be recalled, had also been professor of logic and rhetoric, as well as president of Columbia. How the conscientious Moore was able to budget his time and live, must be an open question; he would have been less than human if he had not found his academic duties, close to home and kin, more congenial than his far-flung ecclesiastical responsibilities, arduous in the extreme. Bishop Moore was a faithful pastor and shepherd of his larger flock. Nevertheless, he was neither a Church nor a Columbia immortal.

During the yellow fever epidemic of the 1790's Benjamin Moore could not have been more devoted, and at the risk of his life. Grandmother Clarke was rightly proud of him. She wrote her sister, Lady Affleck of fashionable Grosvenor Square, London, how her son-in-law had said the last rites for the dead, with only two other clergymen to help him. Many fever-stricken bodies were laid to rest in the churchyard of Trinity. A tenth of the population died; 2,500 were buried in Potter's Field, a burial ground for the homeless.

In July 1797, Clement Moore's father conducted the funeral of "An Amiable Child," as his tombstone near Grant's Tomb testifies to many an interested, if curious, passerby to this day. It has been believed that St. Clair Pollock, just five years old, lost his life by a fall from a cliff, but it would seem to be a safe guess that yellow fever claimed him with so many others.

Clement Moore's grandmother died shortly after the epidemic. She should be remembered. Mary Stillwell Clarke was of the type of Abigail Adams, wife of John Adams, and of other strong-minded women of her time. But she took "the wrong side" in the Revolution and never surrendered. So far as we can tell she was an unreconstructed Tory all her days. She kept her views, however, discreetly to herself after her daughter married the young cleric of Trinity.

To the end of her life, Grandmother Clarke carried on a vigorous correspondence with relatives abroad. Her last will and testament is an interesting paper. She bequeathed a thousand pounds to her son Thomas, and fifteen hundred to her daughter, Lady Mary of England. She provided for the children of her deceased son Clement. To Daughter Charity and her husband, Benjamin, and "to their heirs in fee," she left Chelsea House "and that part of the farm . . . at Greenwyck, called Chelsea and all the buildings and improvements thereon erected. . . ." To them also she bequeathed a Jersey "Salt meadow." Four of her slaves would be theirs outright: Thomas and his wife Ann, Charles, and Hester. Slave Richard she wished put to a trade and supported. When "of full age," he should be freed. Slave Rachel she ordered sold at once. Eventually, it is clear, Clement Moore's Grandmother Clarke intended that her property should pass to him, Charity's only child. The estate he thus inherited included not only Chelsea but also a very large piece of land in "the patent of Kayaderosseras" in upstate New York. This patent was originally some 400,000 acres granted to thirteen prominent citizens in 1708. It caused much unfavorable criticism since it comprised most of a whole county—Saratoga—and parts of three others. The Moores were among the families that invested in this large tract, styled "Queensborough" by the proprietors.

Clement C. Moore was thus not only an accomplished scholar in Hebrew, but also a landed gentleman, a wealthy young man—potentially, at any rate. He did not bury himself wholly in his books. He branched out in several directions. Very early he ardently espoused the Episcopal faith he had received through inheritance, but he determined to study it independently for himself. His first venture in polemics was not very successful. The Honorable Samuel Osgood, former postmaster in Washington's cabinet, was a Presbyterian who took his church affiliation as seriously as young Moore did his, and ventured to explain it in a paper entitled *A Letter to a Young Gentleman.* It was mild enough and presented the Presbyterian argument on church polity lucidly and well.

The scholar of Chelsea took time out in 1807 from his laborious work on the new lexicon to write a rejoinder to Osgood, which he entitled *To a Young Gentleman of This City.* Osgood was fifty-nine years old, Moore twenty-eight. The pamphlet was signed "Philalethes." Quite likely Osgood had heard all the arguments that Moore advanced for episcopal church government, that is, the "laying on of hands" by bishops duly consecrated in apostolic succession. Osgood had been a divinity student, but ill health had obliged him to give up his studies. So far as we know, this passage at arms between Columbia and Harvard was not encouraged by the former cabinet officer. Clement C. Moore remained an Episcopalian; Samuel Osgood, a Presbyterian.

Bishop Moore took his office with his customary fidelity and seriousness, though the Church's adventurous spirit was

Alexander Anderson drawing, courtesy of Columbia University

COLUMBIA COLLEGE IN CLEMENT C. MOORE'S TIME

at a low ebb and he lacked the amazing vitality of his successor, John Henry Hobart. However, he traveled the length and breadth of his vast diocese as much as a not too vigorous physique would permit. He had time, too, for ecclesiastical sword-crossing occasionally when his friend, the impulsive but ably energetic Hobart, needed a champion. He preached constantly. Some of his sermons were brought together by his son Clement and published in two volumes. They are not distinguished. There are no fresh angles of approach to his themes. They are in keeping with the injunction in the preface to the American Book of Common Prayer: "This Church is far from intending to depart from the Church of England . . . further than local circumstances require." Clement Moore was of like mind all his days, a devoted layman whose conscientious discharge of his duties derived from no stranger.

Even within what we should call rather restricted, self-imposed limitations, duty, if carried through, year after year, can be a severe taskmaster. Bishop Moore deeded his estate to Clement in 1809. He had enlarged it to the south of the Clarke holdings. In 1789 he had purchased sixteen acres from James Rivington, a Colonial printer of dubious renown. This New York editor could dip ink from either of two bottles, always to his own advantage. He had acquired the land from one David Campbell by a "strict foreclosure." Earlier owners dated back to the Dutch era. Chelsea now extended south to about the present Nineteenth Street, between the same east-west boundaries.

An urgent call came to Chelsea House in 1804. General Alexander Hamilton was dying at the Jane Street home of the Moores' friend and distant relative, William Bayard, prominent citizen of the day. At Weehawken, no less a person than Vice-President Aaron Burr had wounded Washington's secretary of the treasury in a duel "on the field of honor." What made the summons more poignant was the fact that both

Hamilton and Burr were well known to Chelsea House. Hamilton had been a Trinity vestryman. Burr was within the family circle through his marriage to a cousin of Aunt Maria's titled husband, the Viscount Barrington. Dr. Moore had first heard of Alexander Hamilton when the youth held forth while President Myles Cooper slipped out of King's College door in 1775.

The stricken Hamilton wished to receive the last rites of his Church. He hoped the request would not seem improper. The Bishop could hardly refuse him the bread and wine, but he deemed it wise to read him a homily on dueling. Hamilton replied that if life were spared he would do all in his power to wipe the evil out. He solemnly declared that he bore no ill will toward Burr; he had met the colonel with a fixed resolution to do him no harm. He forgave him all. At two on the afternoon of July 12, Alexander Hamilton died with his friend and Bishop at his bedside.

Though Moore's brother William was an eminent physician he was unable to restrain the Bishop in major activities. Dr. William Moore was a graduate in medicine at Edinburgh, and had a wide practice. For years he had served as a Columbia trustee. In 1811 the Bishop suffered a stroke which left him paralyzed and incapacitated. Five years later, 1816, he died. Bishop John Henry Hobart paid him a moving tribute: "He lives in the memory of his virtues. He was unaffected in his temper, in his actions, in his every look and gesture." Memories of a noble spirit must have flooded back as Clement C. Moore stood at the grave on the south side of Trinity Churchyard only a few feet west of the spot where the Bishop had read the committal words in 1804 over Hamilton's grave.

Clement Moore's *Lexicon,* to return a moment, was never an outstanding success, but it had the distinction of being the first published in America. Not intended to be a scholar's authority, it was rather a textbook for beginners. From the pedagogic aspect it is still worth perusing. Moore believed in a progressive presentation of Hebrew from the simplest to the advanced forms. Memorization, while naturally desirable, must be followed closely, or, better, accompanied by adequate illustrations from the text.

Circumstances beyond Moore's control or expectation withheld the fullest recognition of the merits of his *Lexicon* at the time of its publication; they have since been equally limiting. He had put an enormous amount of time on it—his "heart's blood," as an Old Testament scholar states—and yet, this professor "doubts if as many as one teacher in 50" has even heard of the *Lexicon* by name. Another observer calls the book not so much a lexicon as a "vocabulary with translations," with "some attention to derivatives." The work lacked novelty, originality, except as a textbook. However, it may well have served a useful purpose by stimulating Old Testament learning at Andover, Massachusetts, the principal center of Hebrew studies in the early nineteenth century. It may also be that it had some influence on the work of the distinguished Hebraist, Josiah Willard Gibbs of Yale.

Whatever we think of the *Lexicon,* this can be said: Clement Moore's knowledge of languages, modern as well as ancient, was wide and thorough. He was deeply versed in Greek and Latin. He knew French and German well and had studied Italian under the celebrated Lorenzo da Ponte. While busy with his *Lexicon* he helped a young friend, John Duer, a former student in Alexander Hamilton's law office. Duer asked Moore to write an introduction to his translation of the "Third Satire" of Juvenal. When the book appeared several of Moore's own poems were included, some of them original, some translations.

The Chelsea scholar's translation of the "Chorus" of *Prometheus* by Aeschylus is of particular interest because of its religious import. The sea-nymphs address Prometheus chained to the rock in punishment for having brought fire down from heaven against the will of Jove, even as Adam and Eve had been driven out of the Garden for eating of the fruit of the forbidden tree. A part of the chorus follows, as Moore put it into English:

> Oh may no thought of mine e'er move
> The vengeance of almighty Jove!
> N'er shall my incense cease to rise,
> Due to the powers who rule the skies,
> From all the watery domains
> O'er which my father Ocean reigns:
> And till his towery billows cease
> To roll, lull'd in eternal peace.
> Ne'er shall an impious word of mine,
> Irreverence mark to power divine.
>
> Lightly flew my former days,
> With not a cloud to dim the rays
> Of Hope, which promis'd peace to fend,
> And golden pleasures without end.
> But what a blast now mars my bliss,
> Prometheus, at a scene like this;
> While thus thy tortures I behold,
> I shudder at the thoughts so bold,
> Which could compel thee to withstand
> For mortal man, Jove's dread command.
>
> Where now the aid from mortals due
> For all thy deeds of love so true?
> Alas! their shadowy strength is vain,
> As dreams which haunt the fever'd brain;
> Ah! how should fleeting shades like these
> Resist almighty Jove's decrees?

Such thoughts will rise, such strains will flow,
Prometheus, at thy bitter woe.
How different was the strain I sang,
When round thy bridal chamber rang
The voices of the choral throng,
Who pour'd the hymeneal song
To thee, and to thy joy, thy pride,
Hesione, thy blooming bride.

John Dryden, bright star in English seventeenth-century letters, was Moore's master; yet his *Virgil* gives hardly much greater charm than Moore's "Chorus" from *Aeschylus*. Not until Elizabeth Barrett Browning's *Prometheus* in 1850 do we find a superior to the Chelsea poet's translation so far as catching the original spirit is concerned. For Moore's feeling for the Greek was sensitive and sure; he had a clear understanding of the original and clearly conveys it to the reader.

Not until William Cullen Bryant's translations of Homer did American men of letters show much interest in popularizing the ancient classics. In the America of the early 1800's few scholars of repute gave a thought to rendering a Greek masterpiece into English. We look far before we see so acceptable a translation as Moore's "Chorus." The Chelsea scholar might have started a trend toward English renderings of Greco-Roman works on the order of the Loeb Classical Library.

None of his translations from any language was calculated to attract a wide public. But even one of the most famous translators, John Florio, who gave Montaigne's *Essais* their English dress, could say that this was a "defective edition." He looked upon himself as a mere "fondling foster-father" who often labored "with a jerke of the French *Iargon*." This might be said of Moore's translation from the French of a

James Sharples portrait, courtesy of City Art Gallery, Bristol, England

CLEMENT CLARKE MOORE IN 1810

book originally published in Paris. He called it *A Complete Treatise on Merino and Other Sheep*. It is a compilation by a French author, Alexandre Henri Tessier. The work poses a problem and raises a question. The problem concerns the appendix where Francis Durand is named as "Proprietor and Translator," though Moore wrote his name as the translator on the copy he presented to the New-York Historical Society. He may have felt that he had so thoroughly revised Durand's work as to make it his own. The question concerns Moore's interest in sheep raising. Did merino or any other kind of sheep ever nibble the grass of Chelsea? We do not know. In 1811, the year the translation appeared, there was as yet plenty of grass and plenty of room; it was several years before the city criss-crossed the Moore acres with streets and avenues to help ease the "traffic jams" of the day. It may be that Robert R. Livingston's introduction of merino sheep at "Clermont," his estate in Dutchess County on the Hudson, encouraged Moore's experiment in Chelsea. Sheep-raising had become popular as well as profitable.

The year of this French translation was a busy one for Clement Moore. Though sorely tried by his father's stroke and inactivity the young man, now thirty, sat to James Sharples who vied with Gilbert Stuart in popularity as a portrait painter. Sharples was able to catch the inner self as well as the features of his subjects. For some unexplained reason Chelsea House did not retain possession of the portrait. It is now in the City Art Gallery of Bristol, England.

CHAPTER FOUR

Love, Marriage, Life Work, and Other Interests

THE YEARS of devotion to the *Lexicon* were punctuated by affairs of the heart as well as others of the mind. The young scholar of sheltered Chelsea did not go un-noticed by the belles of New York. There were invitations to parties, balls, picnics; but so serious a young man must have seemed difficult, a bit pompous at times. In reply to a young lady who had asked him "to make one of a party of pleasure into the country" he wrote:

My ear still vibrates with thy sweet command . . .
Still, tremulous, I hold thy parting hand;
I see thee smile still witching me away;
Yet must this willing heart still disobey.
Yes, lovely tempter, yes, I must forego
A transient bliss that leaves a lasting woe.
In shades I dwell where each severer Muse,
And thought, and silence, spread their pallid hues,
But when I bask beneath the melting rays
Of joyous rosy light that round thee plays,
At thought of these my solitary shades,
A chilling horror all my frame pervades.
The Graces that around thee lightly trip,

The Joys that laugh upon thy ruby lip,
The fluttering Loves that, watchful to beguile,
Direct thy glance and lurk beneath thy smile,
They mar my soul for contemplation's powers,
For learning's rugged paths and weary hours,
For deep research that strains the mental eye,
And daring thoughts that soar beyond the sky.
Glide on, sweet maid, in pleasure's gilded barque,
Still blithe and tuneful as the morning lark;
Still let the melting music of thy tongue
Delight the old and captivate the young;
Still, laughing, lead along the sportive train
Whose breasts can feel no deep-devouring pain.
But Oh! if e'er thou mark some gentle youth,
In whose fond breast dwell loyalty and truth,
Let not a conquest's momentary bliss
Tempt thee to trifle with a heart like this.
The breast which generous love and honor swell
Is sacred as the fane where Angels dwell:
The sacrilege that tempts its holy fire
Fails not to rouse a guardian Spirit's ire.
Go now, and may thy heaven-attemper'd mind,
Ere long, some pure congenial spirit find;
Some swift ethereal soul, that shall delight
To chase and take thee in thy wildest flight.
Nor let thy flights and frolics chase away
All thought of him who pours this parting lay;
Whose bosom, mingled pains and tumults swell
While thus he bids farewell—a sad farewell!

Another young lady thought she would prove her interest
in Clement Moore by writing his name "in the sand of the
seashore." Just where the seashore was is not in the record.
But, ah me! When Clement saw the script all he did was to
jot down his feelings in a few lines of uninspired verse:

This name here drawn by Flora's hand
Portrays alas! her mind;
The beating surf and yielding sand
Soon leave no trace behind.
But Flora's name shall still abide
In many a bosom trac'd,
Not e'en by time's destroying tide
Nor fortune's storms effac'd.

It took time for the girls to learn that Clement Clarke Moore was not to be had for the seeking, however coy they might be. When he received an invitation to a ball he gave answer once again in verse:

Full well I know what direful wrath impends,
From Fashion's gay and numerous host of friends,
O'er all who blindly list not in her cause,
Nor swear eternal fealty to her laws . . .

But, he pleaded:

A Vision stood distinct before my sight . . .
"Hail Youth! In me behold a friendly power,
Nor let these warnings, by your Guardian giv'n,
By winning pleasure from your thoughts be driv'n . . ."

Back of all this playful attitude lay a depth of feeling far greater than the immediate romantic occasion. We may note it in "Lines Addressed, Many Years Ago, to the Fashionable Part of My Young Countrywomen." Time had changed his viewpoint though he would not admit it, preferring to maintain that it was rather the "Fashionable Part" of his countrywomen that had changed.

Ye blooming nymphs, our country's joy and pride,
Who in the stream of fashion thoughtless glide; . . .
Yet think not envious age inspires the song,
Rejecting all our earth-born joys as wrong.

Think me no matron stern who would repress
Each modern grace, each harmless change of dress; . . .
But in those half-rob'd bosoms are there hid
No thoughts which shame and purity forbid? . . .
O Modesty and Innocence! sweet pair
Of dove-like sisters! still attend the Fair! . . .

In due time, his own good time—or was it really his after
all, but rather hers?—Clement C. Moore ceased fencing with
"the Fair." He finally met a young lady with every require-
ment of heart, mind, and spirit. How completely he fell in
love may be seen in the "Biography of the Heart of Clement
C. Moore," which he did not publish; it is today in seven
neatly written pages among the papers, few but fascinating,
that adorn the library shelf of the New-York Historical Society. The poet left no deeper revelation of himself than in
these lines, undistinguished otherwise; they were penned for
one purpose only—"to commemorate his marriage to Catharine Elizabeth Taylor on November 20, 1813."

Minerva . . .
When, as her bright eyes roll'd around,
To cast for e'er a farewell glance,
She saw a trembling youth advance;
"O! stay, most injur'd Goddess, stay,
"Nor let thy suppliant vainly pray. . . . "
She stay'd to lead the enraptur'd youth
Through every winding maze of truth:
And had the auth'ress of this rhyme
Some portion of her power, and time,
The inquiring eye should here have view'd
The plans she with the youth pursu'd.
Suffice it, years most swiftly ran;
And when the boy was lost in man,
French and Italian he could speak,

As well as Hebrew, Latin, Greek;
Whilst, treasur'd in his well-stored mind,
Was learning by good sense refin'd,
He shone not with the fire-fly's light,
Which shows itself in flashes bright,
But with the glow-worm's steady ray
The constant lustre of the day.
Needless to say, that love
His breast with passion did not move.
Perhaps the God, with careless eye,
Forever might have pass'd him by;
Grown heedless by unbounded sway,
E'er left him with his guide to stray;
E'er left him with a harden'd heart
Fill'd with contempt for woman's art,
Had not Minerva's pointed quill
Arm'd him with all a poet's skill
Full many a brilliant page to swell
Against Love's officer—a Belle. . . .
The angry Goddess vainly strove
To shield him from the shafts of Love. . . .
She tore him from that dangerous street
Where beaux & beauties duly meet;
She tore him from the giddy town,
That Nature's charms his breast might own,
Hoping they would the mist dispel
That arm'd with charms a fluttering belle. . . .

Presently,
. . . with beam of joy, she found
His tongue with chains of silence bound
Upon that subject which opprest
With grief and pain his troubled breast;
And whilst the wond'ring giddy crowd

Thought he to learning only bow'd,
With heart of flame and looks of snow,
With thoughts of love and studious brow,
Those fires which can the coldest melt,
Unheeded, he in secret felt;
For Cupid, to his eye, array'd
With every charm the worshipp'd maid,
Whilst Wisdom's handmaid, Modesty,
Whisper'd to him, not worthy he
Of daring to such charms aspire,
Daring to show his bosom's fire.
Now Pallas saw, with joy, that time
Had robb'd him of his youthful prime:
For she had hop'd that riper years
Would banish all her cares and fears;
Hop'd that in his maturer age
Again she should his heart engage.

A year, the God, with deepest guile,
Had left him to enjoy her smile
But that he might more fully prove
The sov'reign power of mighty Love;
For doubly painful is the dart
That enters the long sleeping heart.
Late from his guardian's favorite isle, . . .
A youthful, giddy, flirting maid,
Had come, he Cupid's plans to aid
With sparkling eye, with rosy cheek,
With tongue that loved full well to speak
In ev'ry way that best could tell
She was a laughing-loving belle.
Ah! who could dream this fluttering fair,
This outcast from Minerva's care
Could make her pupil heave a sigh,

And fill with love his thoughtful eye?
But, though it ne'er was dreamt nor thought,
Such was the wonder Cupid wrought.

The Goddess, fill'd with lasting hate,
Now left him to his dreadful fate; . . .
When she withdrew her guardian care,
His passion he would then declare,
And that, soon settled as his wife,
The fluttering belle, would rule for life.

Miss Taylor, "the fluttering belle," was nineteen, Moore's junior by fifteen years. As the verses suggest, she had a God-given sense of humor; perhaps this spells the reason for her conquest. That she made other girls jealous we may be sure, for they twitted her and wanted to know how she could possibly fall in love with a man so much older than herself. At long last, for the family's eyes alone, she wrote out her answer in a poem entitled "Clement C. Moore—My Reasons for Loving." Simple, adolescent charm is in every line; love and pride in her choice unaffectedly glow in word upon word.

It has often been said that Catharine Elizabeth Taylor's father was Chief Justice William Taylor, of Jamaica, British West Indies. Search of the records in the Islands as well as in the London Colonial Office yields little if anything to bear this out. Her forebears on her mother's side were of a long line of Dutch-descended citizens of New Amsterdam and of New York. Among them prominently were Stephanus Van Cortlandt, Mayor of the city in 1677 and 1687, and Jacobus Van Cortlandt, his brother, a wealthy, civic-minded merchant. In 1697, King William III granted Stephanus a patent which made him a manor lord of an estate stretching ten miles along the Hudson River north of New York City. It was from this great acreage that the now famous Van Cort-

Courtesy of the Moore Family

CATHARINE TAYLOR MOORE

landt Park in the Bronx was developed as a playground and recreation field for the city's millions. Another relative was Peter Van Cortlandt, a King's College man of the class of 1758, forty years before Clement Moore's time.

Catharine Elizabeth Taylor—always Eliza in the family circle—became Clement C. Moore's bride at the altar of St. John's Church on aristocratic Varick Street. Moore's friend, Bishop Hobart, officiated. St. John's was Eliza's parish church and Clement affiliated with it until they attended St. Mark's Church In-the-Bouwerie a few years later. It was Clement Moore's habit to enter heart and soul into the work of whatever church he joined; at St. Mark's he became a vestryman and a delegate to the diocesan convention over which Dr. Hobart presided. The rector, Dr. Henry Anthon, was a brother of a beloved professor at Columbia, the distinguished Charles Anthon, famous for his long-lived Latin grammar. Moore took particular interest in the music at this historic church which stood, and still stands, on the site of Peter Stuyvesant's chapel. Long afterwards, St. Mark's invited the Poet of Chelsea to come over and test the organ to see what might have to be done in the way of repairs.

Before his marriage Clement Moore had revealed a strong political bent and continued to fan his flair for controversy as his father had rather mildly shown his, though, as a rule, only when friendship urged him.

Clement wrote two pamphlets to show Thomas Jefferson how wrong a great statesman could sometimes be. The Chelsea pamphleteer took particular exception to the President's *Notes on Virginia,* which were republished in 1801 after a lapse of nearly thirty years. Though much had happened since their first appearance, the *Notes* were as abhorrent to Moore as he believed they must be to many who were not courageous enough to talk back or were not inclined to disturb the uneasy peace before the outbreak of the War of 1812.

The Virginian's words, his "infiidelity conveyed in so insidious a manner," stemmed from Voltaire and Rousseau. England had been too stunned by their "infernal yell" to hear the feeble voice of Jefferson, or somebody overseas, thought Moore, must surely have answered him. Now, America must hear that "yell," and who better fitted to reply than Clement Moore himself? For Jefferson was President of the United States, in a position of influence, the reputed guardian of American rights. Thousands of people innocent of what the *Notes* really meant would be reading them in time—many who had never heard of the infidel French philosophers at all.

Jefferson's "snips of learning," as Moore contemptuously styled the Virginian's considerable erudition, and his "show of reasoning," were dangerous and should not go unnoticed. They might be misunderstood as speaking the sentiments of the whole country. America must have an apologist, and Clement Moore elected himself to that high office. But he was modest enough about it, and of course pious. He prayed that "the Searcher of hearts" would support him in his attempt to set his fellow-countrymen right on Mr. Jefferson and his nefarious, irreligious doctrines so cunningly phrased in his *Notes on Virginia*.

Moore was particularly anxious that Thomas Jefferson's views on the Bible might not prevail in America. The President's opinion that mountains had been formed first in the week of creation perturbed Clement. It was false if Holy Writ were right. Turn to Genesis and read: "And God said, Let the waters under the heaven be gathered together unto one place, and let the dry land appear; and it was so." We can almost see the last four words underscored.

Then, there was Jefferson's observation on shells—petrified 15,000 feet above sea level. From this the statesman-philosopher-scientist-biblical expositor boldly, presumptuously, framed his own idea of the Deluge, let Scripture say what it liked. To be sure, Mr. Jefferson did express wonder over the natural processes—as he saw them; but it was a wonder not derived from the Bible, retorted Clement Moore. The "immediate agency of the Almighty" was the correct inference from Holy Writ—no matter what any man might discover through mortal eyes. The humble Christian, Jefferson's critic concluded, needs no "strata . . . and cockle-shells" to make him wonder and believe. He is fortified by the "united voices of all the nations upon the globe." He has a great chorus to testify to this. Let no one doubt it for a moment.

Chelsea's scholar shifted to his own scholarly ground when he struck out against Jefferson's notions about languages. How absurd, he emphatically declared, to say that there had been twenty dialects among the savages of America and the inhabitants of Asia! It was a clear-cut denial of Bible truth! Within the decade past, in 1797, to be exact, so great a scholar as Benjamin Smith Barton of Pennsylvania had substantiated the Biblical account of the origin of language. Read his monumental work, Mr. Jefferson, his *New Views of the Origin of the Tribes and Nations of America*. Sufficient proof is there to refute Thomas Jefferson and all his infidel admirers!

"If but a few among men of talents would devote their spare hours to the attainment of true knowledge, and join hand and heart together," Moore was persuaded, "they might in time become a Spartan phalanx, which would, at least, make a noble, if not a successful stand against the barbarian host, who, it is to be feared, are silently plotting to throw off the restraints of religion, and to tear down the essential principles of government."

To Moore attempts to divorce the political from the moral and religious were futile. They were of one piece. Jefferson's moral and religious views simply must color his politics and his thoughts on the nature of the state.

Not long afterward, the Chelsea economist, religious and

political philosopher, extended his criticism to Jeffersonian ideas on foreign trade. As a good Federalist he had his misgivings on the embargo against Britain. "The contests which engage nations as well as those which arise between individuals," Moore argued, "are frequently concerning objects unworthy of the dangers to which they expose the contending parties. . . . While our government is engaged in a commercial dispute with Great Britain, concerning our foreign carrying trade, every art is employed by our popular leaders to extend and strengthen . . . infirmities incident to the human mind. . . ." One of these infirmities was a certain uneasiness, an apprehension, at the root of the whole question. Wisdom alone could dispel it. "Blindness of passion or romantic jealousy of national honour"—never!

Moore was convinced that the commerce of a nation might be exaggerated as the particular concern of government, whereas the improvement of the soil should be first. Commerce may make men rich but not more patriotic. "The territory we possess is so immense, and so thinly inhabited, as to afford room for the most rapid increase of population which the nature of man will admit and to an incalculable extent of time." With every variety of climate and so vast a territory, America must continue to be "a field so ample . . . as the heart of man could desire, for the beneficial employment of all the capital and industry of its inhabitants."

Worse than anything else, commerce destroys that "sober virtue" which makes a nation great. "The inordinate desire of gain which prevails among us seems excited in order to counterfeit the designs of Providence." In placing our country at such a distance from the theatre of European warfare, the Almighty had "apparently intended that we should never be drawn in to take a part."

But, he reflected, "there is no bound prescribed to the folly and avarice of man." They who worship no God but Mammon, who discourage general industry and the internal commerce of their country, who pay so little respect to truth and equity in their private affairs that an old-time merchant would have had no dealings with them, and who through their nefarious conduct entangle us in a dispute with Great Britain, the one power capable of doing us most harm—these "unprincipled adventurers" had now the effrontery to call upon the nation "to rise and put forth all its power in their behalf!"

The vast mass of his fellow-countrymen were living virtuous lives. Moore was sure of it. Never mind how travelers distorted the picture when they got home. We were not all "tavern-keepers, stage-drivers, boatmen . . . rabble senators and merchant kings." The American people were intrepid and enterprising beyond all others. They showed a zeal for freedom greater than for life itself. Every principle and every interest aroused their patriotism. Nevertheless, "powerful temptations to evil" might make them not very different from men in all ages. Let us not permit the great body of our citizens "to catch the flame of passion." Let them rather "reflect the light of truth." If we fail in this, war might break out, and all must change for the worse. Our leaders would then pursue a course which "nothing but madness could excuse."

"The laws of our actions are plainly set before our eyes," Moore eloquently concluded, "the consequences are in the hand of that overruling Providence to whom, in discussions which deeply affect the interests of nations, the mind of the most thoughtless seems involuntarily to look up for assistance; whose mysterious counsels baffle the designs of the most sagacious; and whose operations elude the vigilance of the most clear-sighted. And may He continue to bless our country, may He give our rulers wisdom, and render her children 'kind and natural,' while other nations are harassed by war and desolation may they still cast their eyes toward her and exclaim:

> 'Thy walls, remote from hostile fear,
> Nor the loud voices of tumult hear,
> Nor war's wild wastes deplore,
> And in thy courts, with lavish hand,
> There smiling plenty takes her stand,
> Has pour'd forth all her store.' "

When the Second War with England broke out, Moore wrote another pamphlet entitled *Addressed to the Citizens of the United States Without Distinction of Party*. Moralist and political philosopher were one as before. It cannot be said that his English descent motivated his pen. He fully realized the nature of "Mr. Madison's War." Of one thing he felt certain: True progress never comes by the sword. "Let us then have peace upon any terms short of dishonour," he fervently prayed. "This war, though not the only ill we suffer, is the great crying enormity which ought at once to be arrested." He took his text from Isaiah—the very familiar sentence: "And he shall judge among the nations, and shall rebuke many people: and they shall beat their swords into plowshares, and their spears into pruninghooks: nation shall not lift up sword against nation, neither shall they learn war any more."

It was France, Moore was convinced, which had induced President Madison to believe what was not the truth about Great Britain. An indirect slap, of course, at Mr. Jefferson's French leanings. With intent the pro-Jeffersonians had spread it around that Britain was "the dupe of French duplicity." And this, Moore reflected, "our government thinks deserving of the smiles of Heaven!" France, infidel and arrogant, had become an obsession. As usual, our pamphleteer ended on a lofty key: "There is no reason to suppose that this nation is to be forever exempt from the changes and

I.M. Scott Esq.

Capt. Clarke

The Monument

CAPTAIN THOMAS CLARKE'S CHELSEA ESTATE AS IT APPEARS
ON THE B. RATZER MAP OF 1767

calamities which have been the lot of all other nations . . . "
Bickerings would arise as the "necessary attendants of a free
government; they would be productive of no lasting mis-
chief; and our body politic . . . might, by temperance and
prudence, arrive at a good old age."

Never again was Clement C. Moore so wrought up as in
this second decade, before his marriage. Never again did
France become so great a bugaboo in his eyes. Eliza exer-
cised a calming influence. Though he flared forth once more
over the nearer issue of the division of his estate by a north-
south avenue, he learned to accept it even to the destruc-
tion of an apple orchard and a walnut grove he highly prized.
And it was while De Witt Clinton, a fellow-alumnus at Columbia, was Mayor of New York that this happened. The
state legislature appointed a three-man commission to plan
the city's future, and, to make matters more difficult, one of
the three was Clement's father's classmate at King's, Gouverneur Morris, able and eminent constitutional lawyer. But
maturity had steadied nerves and broadened judgment.

The whole problem of urban expansion has become a familiar one. In Moore's day it was comparatively new. Personal associations, he learned, mattered little where the
public interest was at stake. Manhattan Island north of
Thirteenth Street would be developed on the west side according to an orderly, regular pattern: north-south avenues
and east-west streets—a criss-crossing as it was popularly
called. It could not be foreseen that the city would need
many more north-south than east-west traffic lanes; if it
had been, New York would today have better transit facilities than it enjoys. The two rivers, it was thought, would
take care of lengthwise travel and traffic. They, in fact, did
until the increase of population required such means of
transit as surface trolleys, elevated railroads, and subways.

If Moore had been a practical politician rather than a

philosopher he would have joined Tammany Hall. His friend, John Pintard, distinguished citizen in more ways than one, had helped found the Hall as a literary and social organization for veterans of the Revolution, but when Moore was a youth in his twenties, Aaron Burr, distantly related by marriage, had changed the Wigwam's course and made it an instrument to win elections. Pintard's influence was worth tapping.

Instead of enlisting Tammany's aid, the learned Moore wrote *A Plain Statement, Addressed to the Proprietors of Real Estate in the City and County of New York*. The title alone killed its chances of success. He signed it "Landowner," not too colorful or eye-catching. He had all but reconciled himself to the inevitable—the cutting up and the leveling of his lovely rural acres—when he thought he would take a last fling at fate and see what happened. The "natural inequalities in the ground, when not too great and too abrupt" are, he argued, "among the greatest beauties to be desired or attained." He quoted Sir Walter Scott's *The Heart of Midlothian:* " 'I'm glad to hear there's a hill,' said Jeanie, 'for bouth my sight and my very feet are weary of sic tracks o' level ground—it looks a' the way between this and York as if a' the land had been trenched and levelled.' " Sir Walter was at the height of his popularity but hardly influential in civic affairs in distant New York.

But why go on? A lesson in municipal economy was being taught all unawares: "Private convenience must give way to public good." Clement Moore would not "arraign the integrity of the individuals" who were doing the city's planning. Such a project, he could see, gave men work. This much at least must be put to "the credit of the municipal ledger." He admitted being peeved that the whole scheme was in the hands of a single city official, the street commissioner, who had far too great a say about public improvements.

Eliza must have heard a good deal on this whole matter. Not only did Clement's much loved trees have to go. Fences, too—and at his expense! Later, assessments were added to his tax bills. And there an end? No, work was soon at a standstill and continued to be for a long, long time. When it was resumed, he found he was liable for a third of the cost. To increase the bitterness the whole project called forth, the new thoroughfare remained a sorry sight for years: the new road unpaved, with tree stumps sticking up like so many tombstones in an ill-kept graveyard. The city made no attempt to level the roadway off or dig out old roots and cart them away. The avenue remained almost impassable; nobody cared anything about it officially.

Clement C. Moore had several constructive suggestions. He recommended that the city authorities go to other communities and see how they did this sort of thing. He singled out Philadelphia as particularly worth studying. Youthful experience had left a nostalgic feeling for the city. He thought it might be a good idea to apply to the state legislature to appoint commissioners who would make "the final regulations of the levels of the streets and avenues." Perhaps, he continued, the owners of any property affected would unite in a petition for a "revision of the laws relative to the opening and regulating of avenues and streets."

Through it all Clement Moore kept his perspective and sense of values pretty well intact—and his sense of humor as well. He engaged an expert craftsman to fashion a beautiful set of dining room chairs out of the walnuts that "progress" had sacrificed to the axe. But it may be a question whether the scholar of Chelsea ever agreed with Charles Lamb that there is "a sweet security in city streets."

Clement and Eliza lived on their divided estate without much to worry about except the illness of one or another of the children who came in rapid succession—too rapid for

75

the mother's health and strength, nine in a decade or so. Chelsea House became a merry one not only at Christmastime but every day the year round. Mother Moore, who lived with them, had the good sense to mind her knitting. English travelers like Mrs. Trollope should have visited Chelsea and seen America at its best. If Clement and Eliza ever read this English lady's *Domestic Manners of the Americans* it must have brought a smile to their countenances. There could not have been a happier home than theirs, with grace, charm, serenity, unhurried existence, and money enough to satisfy every want and creature comfort. Servants and slaves afforded the kind of life and living their loyalty could provide. There was wine of several kinds in the cool cellar that Clement put under the old house. He was not a teetotaler—few gentlemen were—but he took his glass as he took everything else, in moderation.

Moore had no qualms of conscience on either slavery or liquor. When the rector of the Chelsea church delivered a sermon on abolition Clement Moore did not raise his voice in protest against the vestry's request that he resign. It was Thanksgiving Day, 1835. A devout congregation came to hear the pastor's special message for the occasion. Give thanks? he asked. Indeed! For what? Why should the black man give thanks? Slavery was repulsive not to him alone but to God Himself as it ought to be to all His earthly creatures.

We do not know if Moore's servants were in church that morning, but their master was. His pew was not far from the pulpit. How free is America anyway? queried the Rev. Thomas Pyne. "The whole civilized world," he boldly concluded, "expects of America that she should cherish the savage and . . . liberate the slave . . . "

The sermon made it very difficult for Clement Moore who was both a warden and the chairman of the new building committee. The original chapel had outlived its usefulness.

People round about Chelsea House were coming to the church in larger and larger numbers. Would men of means—and there were several besides Moore—withdraw their support of the new edifice that had been planned?

Meetings of the vestry were held in Chelsea House because of Moore's illness. All argument failed to budge the rector from his convictions. Slavery, he insisted, was repugnant to the true Christian. "*Ignorance* is the grand support of slavery," he said again as he had said from his pulpit; "the ignorance, I mean, in which the slave mind is kept. . . . Were not these my feelings I should be unworthy of the Pastoral character."

Chelsea lost a wise leader when Mr. Pyne resigned and returned to his native England. It must have been painful for Clement Moore to see him go, for they had been very friendly. He had invited the rector to lecture on Hebrew, Professor Moore's own specialty, at the new General Theological Seminary not far from the church and from Chelsea House.

The mention of the seminary brings up Clement Clarke Moore's lifelong occupation or, rather, vocation. His teaching was as truly dedicated a service as his father's ministry had been. A scholar of Clement Moore's learning and family background must one day teach. But would it be Hebrew or political economy? For years before and after the publication of his *Lexicon* his dabbling in political and economic theory might have made it seem that Hebrew scholarship was to be an avocation or pastime. During his early married life he had continued to translate this and that—Metastasio's "Ode to Nice," for instance.

In the early 1820's, Clement Clarke Moore settled the question of his life work. He accepted an appointment as professor of Oriental and Greek literature at the seminary in what came to be known as Chelsea Square. His initial sal-

GENERAL THEOLOGICAL SEMINARY IN 1846

ary was $750 a year, but this was increased through the years to $2,000. The school had come into being in answer to a felt need. Bishop Hobart had set up a diocesan school in New York and invited his friend Clement Moore to teach Biblical learning and interpretation of the Scriptures. This would seem to have been a voluntary service.

The feeling for a general seminary for the whole Church had persisted and at last taken shape, but not until after many vicissitudes. John Pintard generously helped keep it going. The school finally came to New York, when Jacob Sherred, wealthy vestryman of Trinity, bequeathed a large sum to help theological education, and Clement C. Moore deeded sixty lots just south of Chelsea House. Bishop Hobart merged his diocesan school with the new institution, which was called the General Theological Seminary. But there were still ups and downs. In 1823 Moore gave the new seminary a needed boost when he delivered a noteworthy appeal in Trinity Church for further moral and financial support. It was a very earnest Address from a very earnest man.

A few years later, Professor Moore's plea seemed answered. Trustees, faculty, students, invited clergy, and prominent laymen gathered at Chelsea House. They formed in procession for the laying of the cornerstone of a new Hall—"Old East"—on Chelsea Square. The Rt. Rev. William White, Presiding Bishop of the Episcopal Church, laid the stone and delivered the Address. A hushed assembly of people from Chelsea listened as attentively as the specially invited guests. The aged Bishop lifted his sonorous voice and urged all present to "put up a mental prayer to the Bestower of all good to govern the minds of those who now or who hereafter superintend the studies of the Institution." Fervently he prayed that "they might furnish the gold, the silver, and the precious stones of sound doctrine, to the exclusion of the wood, the hay, and the stubble of human imperfection . . . "

Let us have a glimpse of the Chelsea that saw Clement C. Moore walking with even pace on its streets in these great, stirring days. "We drove down the short hill through a small apple-orchard," Dr. Turner, a professor at the seminary, used to say in wistful reminiscence, "and riding behind the building came round in front of the west entrance. . . . " A row of trees separated the seminary from the broad grounds of Chelsea House. Deep and viscose mud made the place inaccessible in winter except by carriage or horseback. Another pen recollects the "quiet, studious retreat" where "the devotee of learning had naught to distract . . . or call off his thoughts from solemn, weighty studies . . . " It was like a bit of the English countryside where, as George Eliot might say, you could tell it was Sunday by the very feel of it.

Clement Moore did not spend much time in the Hall save for his lectures. He had an ample library in Chelsea House; many works of his father's. He drew books from the New York Society Library. The records of this oldest public library in America show how wide his reading interests were. Not only the erudite books of his specialty interested him but history, biography, fiction, and poetry about equally so. He was greatly attracted to this library; he served on its board and owned a hundred of its shares. His associates were some of the leading citizens of New York.

A few of Moore's seminary colleagues merit a word. His relations with them were cordial and understanding. He may have had not a little to do with their appointment. Bishop Hobart, his friend, had influence in seminary affairs.

Dr. Samuel Hulbeart Turner, an excellent scholar from Philadelphia, taught Hebrew—indeed, he taught every subject in the curriculum. A man of abounding energy, he taught his specialty also at the new Presbyterian University of the City of New York, now New York University. Turner had become so much impressed by German rationalism, even as applied to the higher criticism of the Scriptures, that some self-appointed guardians of Holy Writ tried to tag him as a "higher critic" and therefore dangerous in a theological seminary. He surmounted this and other difficulties of a suspicious era in the history of the Church and lived to a ripe age beloved and respected by generations of students. Clement C. Moore was spared his colleague's travail of spirit; he rode the waves of scientific as well as ecclesiastical storms to a safe haven but without tacking or trimming his sails.

Bird Wilson, also from Philadelphia, was professor of systematic divinity, nearer Dr. Moore's type of churchmanship than Dr. Turner, who was an out-and-out evangelical. Dr. Wilson's father was one of the most distinguished of America's Founding Fathers, a foremost member of the Constitutional Convention of 1787; with Washington and James Madison he might be said to have steered that great body of statesmen to a successful conclusion of their Philadelphia labors. Bird Wilson had been a justice of the Court of Common Pleas for many years before he entered the ministry. Neither he nor Dr. Moore had the ebullient personality of Dr. Turner. All three impressed colleagues and students alike as earnest and sincere and able. Moore and Turner were especial favorites. Wilson's extreme near-sightedness gave him an owlish and unprepossessing look.

It is Gulian Crommelin Verplanck who holds our attention most as we think back on those beginning days of Chelsea Square. He was of an old Dutch family; his ancestral home was at Fishkill, where the Society of the Order of the Cincinnati was organized in 1784. Though remarkable in varied aspects Verplanck was not the one we should pick for the chair he held; nor was he particularly welcome at the seminary. He was one of a coterie of culture that frequented Chelsea House and enjoyed an evening with the Moores: educators, churchmen, lawyers, writers, musicians, physicians, and businessmen. The Moore-Verplanck friendship may have started at Columbia; Gulian, a grandson of the first president, attained an even better scholastic record than Clement. Verplanck had been the most brilliant student yet enrolled. He numbered William Cullen Bryant among his friends.

When Moore suggested Verplanck's appointment he was opposed by no less a person than John Pintard, worldly wise and astute in such matters. He could not see Verplanck as a professor of evidences of revealed religion and moral science, and he was not all wrong. Truly, Moore's favorite had had no specific preparation for the post. In fact his teen-age years had shown little promise of the worthy man he soon became. When he straightened himself out he studied law and in due time saw the seminary's incorporation papers through the Albany legislature. His later career in politics was distinguished.

Clement Moore pushed Verplanck's appointment with the help of Bishop Hobart, who was also able to perceive beyond the surface of things. Verplanck proved to be an excellent teacher and not the least among the scholars of Chelsea Square. When he retired in 1824, he published, to the surprise of his colleagues, though not to Moore's, "Essays on the Nature and Uses of the Various Evidences of Revealed Religion." For keen perception and breadth of view the work reminds us of *The Varieties of Religious Experience* by William James. The seminary was not noted for productive scholarship in those days. Verplanck's publication was a shock to complacency.

It is to Professor Moore's credit that he fought for a man like Gulian C. Verplanck whose "Essays" were something novel in the 1820's. For Gulian Verplanck tried to apply the Christian faith to everyday concerns. Chairs of applied Christianity were then a distant dream. Theological schools had slight interest in the brooding forces at work in society at large. They were insulated from the world. They made little or no impression on their time or place even though the Church was reaching out through the Domestic and Foreign Missionary Society in which Dr. Turner, alone of the seminary faculty, appears to have taken any active interest. Moore seems to have held himself aloof, though some of his friends, clergy and laymen, and men like John Jay and Francis Scott Key, participated in this forward movement. Small wonder that a man of Verplanck's genius made so little impression at the Square.

Clement C. Moore had by this time removed his family from the winter home on lower Broadway to a house nearer Chelsea in Charlton Street. Here he helped establish a new Episcopal church on Hudson Street opposite Grove. St. Luke's became his spiritual home until he finally settled, winter and summer, at Chelsea House. One of the unexpected fruits of his St. Luke's experience was his friendship for a nineteen-year-old carpenter named James Nicholas Wells. The senior warden took a fancy to the young man and was greatly rewarded, for Wells grew in stature. The wooden sign over the door of his shop changed from time to time: "Carpenter" to "Carpenter and Builder" to "Real Estate." In time, he managed Chelsea's business affairs. The firm he founded still manages the Moore property on Manhattan's west side.

The other interest that caught Clement Moore's imagination was the New York Athenaeum. He and other prominent citizens established it in the middle 1820's as an "institution for the promotion of literature and science." It was formally launched on June 10, 1825, in the chapel of Columbia College. In October, fifty-nine associates issued a twelve-page "Address to the Public." Several of these associates may be noted: Peter A. Jay, Clement Moore's Columbia classmate; William Harris, former rector of St. Mark's; Nathaniel Fish Moore, the poet's cousin; and Dr. William James MacNeven, whom General Gates had befriended when he came to America as a refugee from Ireland.

Dr. Harris was elected president of the Athenaeum, which opened its doors in the Columbia chapel in mid-December, 1825. Ladies as well as gentlemen were admitted to its lectures, books, and the learned association it provided. The Associates pledged their services gratuitously, the Moores among the first. They were joined by Samuel F. B. Morse of the University of the City of New York, and by Clement Moore's friends, Professors Charles Anthon and James Renwick of Columbia.

Idealism was rampant. "The wealth derived from commerce may vanish," the "Prospectus" advised the public; "the pride of monied opulence may be checked, but the works of genius, the productions of learning, and the monuments of taste, are indestructible and unfading." But such an enterprise needed the wealth of the Medici to survive. Expenses kept rising even though time and effort were freely given. A merger with the New York Society Library and the recently founded Philharmonic Society was suggested, but the overtures met with no success. Finally, after a decade and a half of glorious life, the New York Athenaeum came to an end. But it was not a total failure. It pointed the way to adult education and showed how far-seeing Clement C. Moore and his friends were, a century and a quarter ago.

There was still another "cause" in which Moore found interest, though negatively and only in a passing-by sort of way. The temperance movement posed a burning public question in the 1820's. It did not enlist the Chelsea profes-

sor's wholehearted support; he seemed puzzled. The tactics
of temperance advocates drew his ire as few "do-gooders"
ever did. In "The Wine Drinker" he is at pains to state the impractical side, which he saw especially; in "The Water
Drinker" he has some cordial things to say. But let us read
his exposition of the extravagant claims of the "Sober Societies," such as the New York State Temperance Society,
founded in 1829:

> As well might you restrain the breeze
> That sweeps the main and bends the trees, . . .
> As strive to make mankind agree
> To lead their lives from turmoil free.
> No lot so low, no mind so meek,
> That will not for excitement seek.
> Nature in bounds unnatural pent
> Will find some new and dangerous vent.
> A while the blood you may restrain;
> But, held too tight, 't will burst the vein . . .

In "The Water Drinker" he had these comforting words:

> Away with all your wine-fill'd casks!
> To atoms shatter all your flasks!
> Pure water! thus if thou dost flow
> With blessings to this world of woe;
> If such the powers that round thee throng,
> Be thou my only drink, my only song!

Oddly enough, the years ahead saw so many grogshops
in Chelsea and other sections of Manhattan that local temperance—really abstinence—clubs were organized to com-
bat their influence among youth. There was a flourishing
Chelsea Section Club on Eighth Avenue, a few blocks from
the site of the Moore homestead. It was inspired not unlikely by the Methodist Church that had come to Chelsea.

Clement C. Moore was never much impressed by organized morality. He preferred the reform that comes of non-glamorous deeds. He showed this notably when he wrote the following few lines after reading of the death of a Sister of Charity, which a New York newspaper recorded. Mary Frances was ministering to the sick in a hospital when she was herself stricken and died in a few hours. Moore wrote, in part:

> The baubles that command this world's esteem
> No resting place within her mind can gain:
> Like idle notes that cross the solar beam
> They serve to make her spirit's course more plain.
> Yes! such this sacred band; such peace is theirs;
> Unchang'd when days shine bright or tempests lower,
> Through life they pass, untainted by its care;
> When death draws near, they gladly hail his power.
> And then, like birds that seek a better clime,
> On swift untiring wing their spirits rise,
> And gladly leave this turbid stream of time,
> To take their homeward progress through the skies.

CHAPTER FIVE

Shadows Fall—
Candles Light Again

GRIEF shadowed Chelsea House in 1828. Little Emily died and left a lonesome place at the fireside. It was only two years when Clement Moore's friend, Bishop Hobart, yielded his life, one might say, on the altar of untiring spirit. Emily had not been very well through her six short years, but her going was a great shock to so close-knit a family. In 1830, her mother was dead. She had suffered from "a disordered frame"; it is not certain what that may have been. The youngest girl, Maria, looked at her mother's still face; she glanced up at Grandmother Moore and with the solemnity of childhood remarked, "Mamma won't speak to me any more, she is gone to a better place . . . "

Mother of a brood of nine, "a mother that could not be excelled," Eliza was the mentor of her husband in all his undertakings. "The most patient, uncomplaining being," as Grandmother Moore wrote Lady Affleck, she told her doctor "that if God wanted to take her he had dealt kindly in not giving her more pain." With the summons at hand, she resigned herself "to the will of her Maker" and "calmly left the world trusting in the Saviour & hoping through Him for the mercy of that God whom she loved & endeavoured to serve to the utmost. She was indeed what a Christian ought to be." And, continuing: "A companion to his heart's wish, an excellent mistress of our household"; her husband's friends had "always found a welcome." Her "mind, manners & excellent understanding gave him reason to be proud, & he was proud of her . . . " They were "a very happy couple, he a most devoted husband now bowed down with sorrow which he endeavours to overcome, but which I fear will not easily be done away."

Clement Moore met these tests of his faith—particularly the last—with fortitude touched with inevitable reflection on the mystery of it all. His oldest child, Margaret, was only fifteen; his youngest, Maria, four; in between were Charity, fourteen, Benjamin, twelve, Mary, eleven, Clement, nine, William, seven, and Catherine, five: motherless now, at a time of life when they needed a mother most. Before the end of 1830 came another blow: Charity Elizabeth died.

Strong as he was in a confident hope, Clement Moore found it difficult to come to terms with death. The sight of his motherless children renewed his grief day by day. Strangely enough, it was an untutored workman who did most for him. One day as Moore was taking a stroll across his quiet acres, he met his coachman, Patrick. They stopped as usual for a chat. Something prompted the professor's casual remark, that life and death are not easy to fathom. "Why, Sir," was the quick reply, "we must all die." The scholar, the poet, the churchman, was taken aback. "I believe," he frankly acknowledged, "that the sum and substance of all that divines and philosophers offer by way of consolation may be found in the few words of this Irishman." Not profound but characteristic of Clement Clarke Moore: simple sincerity and generous willingness to learn from the humblest of men.

Worse than death in its natural course was the tragedy of

February 1833. Eliza's brother, a bank clerk in his early twenties, had been detected forging Professor Moore's signature in a vain attempt to pay off "a set of gamblers." Unable to face the consequences, he swallowed laudanum. Dr. John W. Francis, eminent physician and longtime friend, hurried over to Chelsea House and witnessed such a scene of distress and wretchedness as he had never known before.

Within the decade of the thirties Grandmother Moore passed her ninety-first birthday. In 1838 she died at the Chelsea home where she loved and was loved. Charity Clarke Moore seemed a woman out of old time—so rich in wisdom, so understanding of young married life, so adroit in dealing with childhood and youth, so forthright yet so tenderly sympathetic without gush, without tears apparently. She was the last link with the long past. Clement Moore, who owed much of his stalwart character to this grandmother, would never see her like again. Her letters sparkle to this day. Broad-minded, outgiving, to the close of her life she continued to write to her sister in England. "Reading is still a very pleasing employment to me," she wrote Lady Affleck, "although only a present pleasure, for I remember very little of what I read. Old Dr. Johnson once President of our College said he thought it no loss to forget what he read for, when he took his book again, it was new to him. I cannot say that I am of his mind." In spite of this her reading was extensive; she kept herself acquainted with happenings abroad as well as in America: Lafayette's visit, the British Reform Bill, the Black Hawk War. Her memory was keen to the last. In a postscript to a letter that the poet's eldest daughter, Margaret, wrote her aunt, the old lady of Chelsea added: "Our children have been greatly amused at the Idea of the King's enquiry after me. It does not appear long since I saw him a young midshipman coming up Wall Street an object of curiosity to the gazing multi-

Daniel Huntington portrait, courtesy of the Moore Family
CHARITY CLARKE MOORE

tude pleased to see the King's son." When the Prince of Wales, the future King William IV, to whom she refers, visited America he attended services at Trinity Church. The clergy introduced him to members of their families, including the inimitable Charity.

Moore gradually learned that one secret of overcoming grief lies in work; another, in a widening interest in friends and in what is going on. Oaks, maples, walnuts, sycamores, and alanthus, which were especially abundant in Chelsea, shut off much of winter's snow and shielded the house from winds; in late spring and summer they welcomed the poet to the sunshine their shade invited. He seemed to be more and more conscious of the trees, the shrubs, and the flowers of Chelsea, though we miss the rhapsody of a nature enthusiast. He always enjoyed the robins when they flitted down upon his lawns.

Communion with friends gave greater pleasure than with nature. Former Mayor Hone had a daughter much beloved. He had her head fashioned in marble and asked Moore to come and see it. The visit ended, the guest sent a few lines of graceful verse with a bunch of flowers to the Hone house:

> There is a language giv'n to flowers,
> > By which a lover may impart
> The bitter anguish that devours,
> > Or extacy that swells his heart.

> And all the feelings of the breast,
> > Between the extremes of bliss and wo,
> By tender flow'rets are exprest,
> > Or plants that in the wild wood grow.

> These new-cull'd blossoms which I send,
> > With breath so sweet and tints so gay,
> I truly know not, my dear friend,
> > In Flora's language *what* they say;

> Nor which *one* hue I should select,
>   Nor how they all should be combin'd,
> That at a glance, you might detect
>   The true emotions of my mind.

Mr. Hone replied in verse:

> Fill'd as thou art with attic fire,
> And skill'd in classic lore divine,
> Not yet content, would'st thou aspire
> In Flora's gorgeous wreath to shine?
> Would'st thou in language of the rose
> Lessons of wisdom seek t'impart
> Or in the violet's breath disclose
> The feelings of a generous heart?
> Come as thou wilt, my warm regard
> And welcome, shall thy steps attend;
> Scholar, musician, florist, bard—
> More dear to me than all, as friend.
> Bring flow'rs and poesy, a goodly store,
> Like Dickens' Oliver, I ask for *Moore*.

The Poet of Chelsea kept up a correspondence with friends abroad. When Lord Holland died, his daughter, Lady Lilford of Grosvenor Square, received a heart-warming letter from Chelsea House. It was a model of restraint and chiseled beauty: "Every one whom I have ever heard speak of Lord Holland seemed charmed with his uniform sweetness of temper and gentleness of manners; which, added to the high powers of his mind, must have rendered him indeed a blessing to all his family and friends."

Local social clubs marched through Chelsea's new-made streets on holidays; "chowder parties" grew in popularity. Moore liked to look at the marchers from his window in the new house he had built—it is still standing—at the corner of Ninth Avenue and Twenty-third Street. For some years St.

Patrick's Day parades had been making March 17 different from other days. Dr. Moore took delight in walking over to Eighth Avenue and watching the Irishmen turn south from Twenty-third Street. They were regaled in bright green, of course, and it would not surprise us if Patrick the coachman stood with the poet and applauded with him. For there was a great breadth, sincere and refreshing, in the list of the professor's associates: Philip Hone, former auctioneer and onetime Mayor; James N. Wells, former carpenter, now a real estate operator; Don Alonzo Cushman, former farmer, now well-to-do businessman and banker, who had some of the Moore lots and established his family in style on Ninth Avenue.

The Chelsea household had changed greatly. Mother, Grandmother, Emily, and Charity were dead. Two of the other children had married—Margaret first, then Benjamin. The poet wrote Margaret some moving words in a four-page poem when she became Mrs. John Doughty Ogden. But it was his youngest child, Maria Theresa—beloved Terry—who was his mainstay during these years, though Mary was near and very dear to him. When Terry made a trip to England he worried the whole time she was away. "I am more grateful to Heaven, than words can express," he sighed on her return, well and happy, one October day. He himself never seems to have gone abroad. Terrors of the Atlantic were magnified a hundredfold. And yet it was an age of more and more travel. Speed was a sort of mania in those pre-Civil War years. Yankee clipper ships made the Atlantic crossing comparatively common.

With Terry, the Poet of Chelsea journeyed to Sing Sing from time to time to visit Benjamin and his wife, Mary Elizabeth. He had once contemplated making a summer home on the Hudson. In 1839, he bought a beautiful estate at Sing Sing, apparently from his realty friend, James N. Wells. He let Benjamin have the property and it remained in his family until a few years ago when it was divided, one part for a park, the other for a private-house development. Shortly before Eliza's death Dr. Moore had been thinking of removing from Chelsea to upper Manhattan, possibly to the rural Harsenville section two and a half miles north. He became interested in the Bloomingdale Dutch Reformed church there and subscribed to its pews. So serious was he about removing that he and Eliza went over to New Utrecht, Long Island, to get John Pintard's advice. Eliza's "disordered frame" and death ended the dream. He gave up the idea altogether and stayed in Chelsea to the end of his days.

Several other trips were made in these difficult thirties, and forties too: to Garrison, to West Point, even to far-away Saratoga, which so fascinated him that he wrote his longest poem, in six parts, to commemorate the trip. As has been stated, Dr. Moore had a considerable real estate interest in this section of upstate New York.

In 1848 Mary married her sister Margaret's widower, Dr. Ogden. She lived in her father's house at Newport, corner of Catherine Street and Greenough Place. Moore's visits were usually marked by stop-overs at Hartford to chat with his friend, Bishop Thomas C. Brownell of Connecticut, always friendly to the seminary, or to cheer Eliza's sister, Miss Susan Taylor, a mental patient at her "Retreat." "She is a wretched object," he moaned after one of his visits. The physical condition of his youngest son gave him much anxiety. "I visited my son Clement," we read in the father's diary, "and was much distressed by his appearance. I pray God to show me what I ought to do for him." It may be added that Clement Junior lived to be sixty-eight, a quarter of a century after Clement Senior's death.

Moore's principal interest in these years was still his teaching, to which he was devoted alike from the student as from the scholarly angle. He was an exception among the professors of his day in that he believed that learning should be adjusted to the capabilities of the young rather than to the minutiae of subject matter. Language must interpret literature—in his case, the Bible. Literature should be read to broaden the meaning of life.

It has often been said that we know little about Clement C. Moore as a teacher, that the memory of his work has faded out on Chelsea Square. So far as the memory is concerned it is still vivid, or at least as vivid as of any other teacher. Very likely, he is remembered by as many as recall John Knox at Union Seminary or Solomon Schechter at the Jewish Seminary. A full century has passed. How much can a Columbia man recall of James Renwick or Charles Anthon, two of the foremost professors of Moore's time? And at Yale, except some "old grad," who knows much about William Graham Sumner? Or even the more recent "Billy" Phelps whose fame is a part of campus tradition? And yet, Sumner and Phelps were among Eli's most distinguished professors in the generation of men still living. Clement C. Moore had none of the wit of Sumner, none of the dramatic charm of Phelps.

If Professor Moore had shown glaring mannerisms, some marked peculiarity of speech or gesture, he might be recalled as one of his successors is, who introduced Old Testament worthies as Mr. Adam, Mr. Noah, Mr. Elijah; or a faculty member with a throat difficulty, who punctuated his lectures and even his prayers with a raucous, guttural sound; or another, whose voice was so high as to make him memorable more for his stridency than for the content of what he taught. So far as we know, Clement C. Moore never fell asleep during evensong, to be waked by a kindly tug at his gown.

One story has come down to us from a student who was

an honor man in Hebrew not so long after Moore's day as to make it doubtful. It is not too sparkling but is the best available. "The famous rendering of a Hebrew passage in Micah by one of his students was once a favorite bon mot . . . " this old, old friend told me years ago. "I love justice but clemency more!' " It was a very free, rather banal translation, to be sure, a garbled one, of the famous sentence which the King James Bible construes: "And what doth the Lord require of thee? To do justice, to love mercy, and to walk humbly with thy God."

The tradition persisted long after Clement Moore's death that he was the quintessence of courtesy, courtliness, and gracious manners, that he displayed a rare tolerance of differing opinions—rare, even in present-day lecture-rooms. This is not to say that he suffered fools gladly or let toleration masquerade as tolerance. He was staunch in his belief that the professorial chair required a certain dignity if it would win the respect of students. He was sure that learning is not something opposed to piety, that religion and thought are not at odds with each other. While he was not a higher critic in the iconoclastic sense of some of his European contemporaries, he nevertheless used to say that the Bible "is almost as much encumbered by the friendly efforts of its commentators as harassed by the attacks of its foes." Academic freedom has never been better defined than in his words: "To forbid the acquisition of knowledge, because it may render a man vain, presumptuous, or pedantic, or more devoted to the improvement of his understanding than to the cultivation of his religious sentiments, would be to forego a certain good through fear of a possible evil, to shut one's eyes and grope in the dark, because men sometimes stumble in the light."

We have no doubt as to Moore's pedagogic method. In the introduction to his *Lexicon* he gives specific directions as to how Hebrew should be taught. In an Address at Christ Church in New York he elaborates these directions. He was so modern in his thinking that we are forgetful that the psychology of learning was a term but little understood in the first half of his century. He was more of a professional teacher than a scholar talking. One might not expect to find him lecturing to vacant seats as some foreign professors were known to do.

"It is hoped," observed Moore at Christ Church, "that no student will feel disappointed at finding the mode of learning [at the seminary] carried on in the old-fashioned manner. It seems to be by some imagined, that knowledge may be acquired without any other exertion than the trouble of listening; as though they were vessels capable of receiving and retaining the information poured into them by others. I freely confess my entire ignorance of the manner of effecting this sort of inspiration. It will be expected of the students, directed by the experience of their professor, to acquire what they learn by the exercise of their own faculties and the exercise of their own diligence." No trace of "soft pedagogy" in such a sentence!

Moore's sense of humor comes out in this lecture. "The study of Hebrews is, by many, supposed to be one which cramps the intellect and renders genius dull," he observed. "The words of the satirist have become almost proverbial:

'For Hebrew roots—are found
To flourish most on barren ground.'

Nor is this sarcasm without foundation in truth . . . But . . . there is no necessity to be always occupied in digging among the roots, and clearing away the weeds and brambles . . . Look up and see the 'fragrant flowers and delicious fruit.' "

Professor Moore was not a mere theorist. He conducted his course in "such a manner as to give to the recitation . . .

the character of friendly and familiar conversations, and to afford the students every encouragement to state, without reserve, whatever they found difficult or embarrassing, and to offer freely the thoughts which presented themselves to their minds, in the persuasion that more may be learned by unreserved communications than by formal lectures, and that the lively and unbiased intellects of youth may sometimes produce combinations of ideas, from which even veterans in literature may derive advantage."

We have a few statements in vivid recollection of Clement Clarke Moore as a teacher. His "translucent simplicity and childlikeness, . . . inoffensive and unsuspecting goodness," Bishop William R. Whittingham of Maryland remembered through all of thirty years. Bishop Horatio Potter of New York told Dr. Moore personally how gratefully, how tenderly he recalled his kindness, his "gentle but admirable instruction" and his "lovely Christian character."

But seminary duties did not take up all of Moore's time. He continued deeply interested in church affairs, and particularly as new faces were seen on Chelsea streets. Some had come to escape the yellow fever, others from abroad—Scotland, Ireland, and England principally. By 1830 a community had developed round about Chelsea Square: men, women, and children, many of them tenants of Clement Moore's. Chelsea House no longer felt alone on its cliff above the Hudson. The seminary would soon have a second building—a West Hall, which is still standing. The chapel, it was now felt, must not be for students and professors exclusively. Dr. Wilson and Dr. Turner thought it should be opened to the neighbors, and it was, with a Sunday school for the children. Students and ladies of the faculty served as teachers, Miss Margaret Moore one of them.

In May 1831, a parish was organized with Clement C. Moore as the first secretary. Here was a marked trait of character—willingness to serve in any capacity if it would help the cause. He did not try to dominate the councils of the new parish; he did everything that nobody else could or wanted to do. On seven lots, which he gave, a church building was begun on Twentieth Street between Eighth and Ninth Avenues. When St. Peter's Chapel was finished, he became the first organist. The name was his suggestion, in all probability. St. Mark, St. Luke, St. John, and St. Andrew had all been honored in and about New York, but not St. Peter. Moore drew the parish seal, which depicts a Greek temple on a rock. From the beginning he seems to have dreamed of a larger edifice. He gave up his idea of a Greek basilica when the architect recommended a modified Gothic after the style of Magdalen College, Oxford. Another trait: no overweening pride of opinion.

As Dr. Moore had sat at St. Mark's and St. Luke's vestry meetings, so at St. Peter's—prompt, punctual, quiet, retiring, yet spontaneously ready to contribute of his thought as well as of his means, his time, his energy. As some one observed, Clement C. Moore was "unconsciously pre-eminent" in all things. But he was not invariably wise. He did little to prevent the new parish's going into debt, though he helped Trinity see its way clear to grant a loan, and was one of the guarantors of another loan, from Robert Lenox, a Scottish immigrant now of great wealth.

The debt was the result of a bad guess. Everybody believed that Chelsea must one day be "the court end of town." The vestry of Trinity also believed it. When the struggling St. Bartholomew's on Great Jones Street sought a loan, around the same time as St. Peter's, the Chelsea church was preferred as a better risk. It is ironical when we think of the high estate of the beautiful edifice of St. Bartholomew's on Park Avenue today. Through all the years ahead, to the hour of his death, Clement Moore was the in-

Henry Inman portrait, courtesy of the Moore Family
CLEMENT CLARKE MOORE IN THE EARLY 1840's

spiration of St. Peter's in poor weather and in good. One of the rectors used to say that in every reduction of debt, Dr. Moore was by far the largest contributor—and it would have been no exaggeration to name him "the St. Nicholas of St. Peter's Church as he certainly was in spirit."

Moore's stamina when winds blew a gale showed his character at its best. Let come what might, his dogged determination to complete the new edifice was unremitting. The panic of the late 1830's almost strangled Chelsea as it pleased, but the work must go on. With much ceremony on June 29, 1836, St. Peter's Day, the cornerstone was laid on schedule. The "court end of town" must have the largest church and soon the finest organ that William Erben could build even if it cost $5,000, an unheard-of sum in those days. And yet, the while, the city of a quarter of a million inhabitants staggered: industry stood still, credit tightened, and real estate values tumbled precipitately. Chelsea, nevertheless, enjoyed another great day—the day when the edifice was consecrated to the glory of God and the welfare of men. It was on Washington's Birthday 1838—a day to be remembered. When the doors were opened Dr. Moore led the vestry and congregation to the Latin-numbered pews.

Moore, it will be recalled, had taken a special interest in church music. He had known the organists of St. Mark's, St. Luke's, Trinity, and other churches. He was expert not only at the keyboard but also on repairs. When, as has been stated, St. Mark's called him over to see what might be done with its ailing instrument, he reported in his customary vein of economy: "I was able to get but an imperfect view of the interior of the organ; but I think the mechanism is, for the most part, in very good order . . . " At small expense, it could be made all right.

Clement Moore's interest in organs and organists brought romance to Chelsea. Trinity Church had called the celebrated Edward Hodges from England to serve as organist in the early 1840's. He has been credited with introducing higher musical standards into American churches. Moore's acquaintance with him led to Miss Sarah Ann Moore's. She was a daughter of the professor's Uncle William, and a frequent visitor at Chelsea House. Miss Sarah may have reminded Moore of his Grandmother Charity. She had a brilliant mind, a scintillating wit, and a character humble to poor and rich alike. The Danish sculptor, Thorvaldsen, modeled her lovely head in exquisite marble. According to George Templeton Strong, a Trinity vestryman, the young lady came pretty near causing a serious rift in the household at Chelsea. When her engagement was announced the celebrated diarist called it a misalliance. He thought he saw a certain snobbishness in Dr. Moore. The professor seemed so much displeased that he threatened to quit America and take an apartment amid the Pyramids. Strong could see no reason for this, except that Hodges was not deemed good enough for Moore's favorite cousin.

The facts go to show how far wrong a bright, aristocratic but prejudiced young man can be. Strong did not like Professor Moore. He had met the Poet of Chelsea and several of his children at Sharon, Connecticut, and later referred to them as "Clement Moore & Co." The sons were just beyond Strong's understanding, even worse; but the girls were very nice. George Templeton Strong was twenty-eight and a bachelor.

It was at a Chelsea House window one day that Miss Sarah first caught sight of Edward Hodges, then a widower with a devoted family. The Trinity organist was standing with her cousin at the gate and about to say good-bye. They seemed so friendly that Sarah ran up to Cousin Clement afterward to inquire who the gentleman might be. "Why, Sarah," Clement replied, "that is the great Dr. Hodges!" So,

Clement Moore did not flee to Egypt. The sister of Columbia's president became Mrs. Hodges—to the delight of everybody, even the organist's daughter, Faustina, who wrote about the match as a great success: her stepmother was one of the most charming of women.

Clement C. Moore was not just friendly toward Edward Hodges. He was closely so. One of his longest poems, five pages, twenty-one quatrains, he called "The Organist." He dedicated it "To my much esteemed and highly gifted friend, Edward Hodges, Doctor of Music." A few of the stanzas will point up their fine relationship. Instead of Virgil's opening lines in the *Aeneid,* "Of arms and the man I sing . . ." Classicist Moore began:

The troubles of an Organist I sing;

—then on to particulars:

His duties and his pleasures too;
Nor is his charge a light and trifling thing,
If to his station he be true.

'T is oft his task, a high and holy end,
By humblest agents, to attain,
To teach th' Almighty's praises to ascend
From whimpering minstrels, pert and vain.

When none but thoughts religious, gentle, kind,
Should reign within the sacred choir,
It is his lot, too often, there to find
Low bickerings, envy, mutual ire . . . . . .

To vex him too, the organ bellows squeak,
Or finest notes get out of tune;
Some pipes seem sulky, and refuse to speak,
While some loquacious, speak too soon. . . .

But when all's done that human pow'r can do
To make his duties smooth and light,
And movements noiseless glide, and notes are true,
Then let him see his *heart* is right . . . . . .

The gifts of Nature, be they e'er so high,
With all that art can teach, combin'd,
Cannot avoid the artist to supply,
The want of a religious mind. . . .

For when, obedient to his skillful hand,
In full accord sweet voices rise,
And holy zeal inspires the sacred band,
He mounts in spirit to the skies. . .

Throughout life Moore kept the gay and the serious in their proper places. Aristotle's middle way, the golden mean, imbued his spirit. He avoided extremes in religion and politics, in family life, and in social affairs. He had something of Emerson's serenity. A good example may be found in his attitude toward the Tractarian Movement which stirred the Church of England to her depths in the 1830's and 1840's. The upsurge of first-century Christian thought, the revival of interest in medieval practices, threw the seminary into an unsettled intellectual and spiritual state. But Professor Moore remained above the dither—calm, unruffled, urbane, apparently unaffected. His influence was great in a critical hour. He was probably sympathetic with the Oxford men who touched old forms and formularies to life, gave fresh meaning to long-held creeds, renewed the ancient glow in sanctuaries. Edward Hodges had sensed this and used it to excellent effect in church services. He won Clement C. Moore as a friend, and with his bride came to live around the corner from Chelsea House.

The Poet of Chelsea also took a long view toward the

destructive forces that the intellectual ferment on the Continent developed. Science and the so-called higher criticism, which declined to exclude the Bible from close inquiry, were befuddling men's minds; the natural scientists in England, the higher critics in Germany. Sir Charles Lyell's studies of the earth's history and structure in the 1830's set a new pattern for the story of man's origin as told in Genesis. Instead of lambasting Lyell, Moore borrowed his *Geology* from the New York Society Library. His interest may have caused him quietly to review his strictures on Jefferson's *Notes*.

Certainly, Clement Moore was not particularly perturbed. Frequent deaths had made him think deeply on first and last things. Nothing is clearer than this as we go through his fascinating diary. Mental illness of relative and friend perplexed him spiritually and practically. What could he do about it? If his religious foundations had not been so securely laid in the old days at Chelsea and Columbia, at Trinity, St. Paul's, St. John's, St. Mark's, and St. Luke's, there is no telling what direction his life might have taken. He was conservative, it is true, not the pedantic scholar that some have depicted him. He kept his windows open to whatever light there was. His very being appears to have woven an intellectual and spiritual robe seamless throughout. Nothing could rend it seriously. He examined new doctrine, new thinking, but it had to square itself with faith, the faith that had sustained his fathers and himself.

It was a trial of no ordinary sort when two good friends, the rectors of St. Peter's and St. Mark's, challenged a former student, a young man of deep conviction and purity of life. How did Arthur Carey stand with regard to Anglican doctrine and practice as they had taught them all their lives? How would he explain—how could he explain—his evident leanings toward the Oxford Movement? Young Carey had read the writings of Pusey, Keble, and Newman, and others

105

of the Tractarians. Their "advanced" churchmanship had impressed him. Dr. Hugh Smith of St. Peter's looked upon the matter with alarm. The youthful candidate for orders was a teacher in the Chelsea Sunday school. At the trial that ensued Drs. Smith and Anthon openly accused Carey of unorthodox teachings. But the Bishop declined to accept their interpretation and further protestation and proceeded to ordain Arthur Carey. Dr. Moore's attitude may be puzzling to some, for he does not seem to have taken sides one way or another. But this was his middle-aged habit in controversy. He wished to temper the winds to a shorn lamb. They were rising high enough at the seminary and, indeed, in the Church at large. Besides, more mundane matters claimed attention.

The cholera epidemic was rampant in these early forties. The medical profession seemed at a loss to know what to do. Chelsea was not immune. The disease had crossed the Atlantic to Canada. At first, it was the cities that suffered most, but the plague moved out to the more rural sections and took a heavier and heavier toll. Since it followed so soon the yellow fever terror, New York, a principal port of entry, continued to be grievously afflicted. So far as we know, Chelsea House was spared, but there must have been many an anxious day and night.

Mr. Wells, the once young carpenter on Hudson Street, was now a real estate man on Ninth Avenue. He did his best to make Chelsea the fashionable section of town. Twenty-third Street must become a thoroughfare. On the advice of Wells, in 1830, Dr. Moore declined an offer of $45,000 for his property. Wells thought the English lease-system better than outright sale of land. Fifteen years afterward William Torrey came up with a project for the first large-scale development of Chelsea. He wanted to build a London Terrace on the Twenty-third Street side of the block between Ninth and Tenth Avenues. On the north side would be single-family, boxlike dwellings; for many years afterward they lent a quaintness to the whole neighborhood. Important tenants were attracted to the Terrace; one in particular is worthy of mention: Mr. Samuel Lord, merchant of Catherine Street and some day the senior partner in the great retail dry goods firm of Lord & Taylor, now on Fifth Avenue. The original Terrace was replaced by another occupying the entire block about twenty-five years ago.

Stagecoaches were soon rumbling along Ninth Avenue from a terminal on the corner of Twenty-third Street where, still later, Jay Gould and others built their Grand Opera House. Chelsea was booming, thanks in great part to James N. Wells, who had grown so portly and distinguished looking as to make passersby often take him for Henry Ward Beecher, strayed from Brooklyn to seek out a pastoral vineyard in Chelsea. Some one named Benjamin Moore, who may have been a relative of the professor's, became proprietor of a stage line from the present Brooklyn Bridge through Chelsea to far-north Manhattanville. Chelsea folk traveled also in swift Knickerbocker stages to rural outlying sections —the present Riverside Park and Morningside Heights, site now of Clement Moore's alma mater.

Moore does not seem to have objected to this development. He had become resigned to change. Years before, we recall, he had resented the city's intrusion, but now he accepted the "progress" of these mid-nineteenth century decades, and let Mr. Wells take over many of his temporal worries. The retail trade was still on Grand Street, but Chelsea shortly had its share of it. The population kept mounting. The decade between 1830 and 1840 had seen an increase of a hundred thousand. Gone were the days of Christmas Eve 1822! None realized it more vividly than the Poet of Chelsea. The avenues, once country roads, were becoming throbbing channels between rows of small, red brick houses. Business was booming everywhere. Moore had foreseen this, or Wells had seen it for him, and purchased a number of acres east of Eighth Avenue, almost to Fifth, recently opened as a promising north-south thoroughfare. For fashion or for trade? No one could predict with assurance. There were signs very soon that *nouveaux riches* would get there first, and they did.

Chelsea had become part of the corporation of the City of New York and was referred to as "uptown" or "downtown." Clement C. Moore could not help being a very rich man. In 1820, he had paid real estate taxes up to $17,000; in 1845, a writer on the New York *Sun* estimated his wealth at $350,000. And yet he may have mused that wealth and progress were poor substitutes for what he missed in his beloved Chelsea—the restful quiet he had enjoyed in earlier days. "For what is a man profited, if he shall gain the whole world, and lose his own soul?" As true of neighborhoods as of men! Clement C. Moore must many a time have felt that Chelsea had come pretty near losing its soul; a man of his tastes and breeding could hardly help thinking that the material had pushed aside the spiritual in one way or another.

Friendship, one might think, would be widened by all that had been happening. When Moore received a letter from a Staten Island acquaintance who wanted to visit Chelsea, they realized that they were living "almost at antipodes to each other." It was not the easiest of trips across New York Bay to Staten Island, even on "Commodore" Cornelius Vanderbilt's speediest ferryboats. Moore's friend would have taken the better part of a morning or afternoon, perhaps the whole day, to reach Chelsea.

In 1847, Vanderbilt dreamed bigger dreams than ever. He applied for a franchise to lay steel tracks straight through Chelsea and run steam trains up the west side of

Manhattan from Chambers Street to Spuyten Duyvil. Vanished forever all that was left of Chelsea's rural loveliness except within the seminary grounds! The new transit facility would strew cinders from locomotive engines along whatever remained of the countryside and oblige Clement Moore to shut his windows. No longer did the big living-room looking glass reflect the green of Chelsea and nothing else. But belching smoke and cinders were not all; freight trains, rackety and long, puffed their way with frequent screeches to warn the track far ahead. An outrider, his flag aloft, waved folks to the sidewalks until the cars had rumbled by. But death spared Clement Moore the worst in transit facilities. In the late 1860's the Ninth Avenue Elevated railroad—the "El"—was rumbling wood-fired locomotives high above the sidewalk, with a station almost at his door.

The sojourner in Chelsea today will find scarcely a trace of the once charming landscape. Only Chelsea Square is left. The marshes are gone, where snipe were plentiful; the woods are gone, where game abounded. Canyons of brick have taken their place. The river front has been pushed out to the west of Tenth Avenue.

CHAPTER SIX

Music and the Arts

THE hard-working clergyman of the fishing village of Brixham, England, had not yet written "Abide with Me," with its moving line, "Change and decay in all around I see," when Clement C. Moore witnessed both in Chelsea. But neither change nor decay dampened his interest in the arts or in the good life generally. He might be trusted to keep within the circle of old-fashioned common sense and join with the best as he interpreted it in the city he loved. The New York of the middle decades had a number of societies of a varied sort, some old, some new.

With Eliza, Clement Moore had doubtless enjoyed many a hearty laugh as they read together Irving's *History* of the Knickerbockers; they could smile at Oloffe Van Kortlandt's "grave" in old St. Mark's. But Moore did not join Irving in 1835 in organizing the Saint Nicholas Society for "ancient New Yorkers." He never became a member of the high-toned Union Club—though several relatives and other "Congenial citizens" were active in this "mother of clubs" in 1836 in the rooms of the Athenaeum Literary Association on Broadway and Chambers Street.

Nor did he journey to see the Scots of the St. Andrew's Society at their Caledonian games. He was not a sportsman in any sense. One could not expect to see him in the cabin of John C. Stevens' yacht or helping this much esteemed gentleman found the celebrated New York Yacht Club in the mid-1840's.

However, in October 1813, the month before he was married, Moore did join the New-York Historical Society, which John Pintard had fathered a decade before. The youthful scholar was not enthusiastic about his membership and gave it little of his attention. Maybe, and not unnaturally, he had no time for it; at any rate, all he did was to give it a book or two. This is no reflection on the great society for, strange as it may seem, the history of New York did not interest our born and bred New Yorker.

But the New York Society Library did enlist Moore's efforts. The library had been established in 1754 when some of his father's friends were engaged with the affairs of the city. Clement Moore became a valued trustee at different times. He contributed copies of his own books and made frequent borrowings. As a reader he was more thorough than rapid. He displayed Grandmother Moore's wide interest—wider in his case than one might think or expect. Architecture and science were well liked, but of course literature, that is, the so-called polite letters, predominated. Irving, Marryat, Drake, De Staël, Sidney, Dryden, were on his list. Poetry and prose, past and present, English, American, and Continental, were favorites. He might even take home a book by that tavern frequenter, Tobias Smollett. He met interesting fellow-borrowers as he browsed at the Society's new building on Nassau Street: former President James Monroe; ex-Governor Morgan Lewis; James Kent, eminent jurist; Cousin Nathaniel Fish Moore, of the Columbia faculty; James Renwick, noted architect; and the businessman James Isaac Roosevelt.

Moore showed no special interest in some of the major

institutions of his time. The New York Public School Society, which his friend De Witt Clinton did so much to establish, did not attract him in the least. The Poet of Chelsea had no part or lot in the rising movement for free public schooling. Horace Mann might have been on a different planet for all Clement Moore knew or perhaps cared. Apparently, Moore did not appear at any of the assemblies of the new public school No. 11, only a few blocks south of Chelsea House.

Union Theological Seminary came to University Place during these active middle years, but Clement Moore restricted his teaching to Chelsea Square. The University of the City of New York was founded on the east side of Washington Square in the early 1830's but while his colleague Dr. Turner affiliated with it, Moore did not. This is not to intimate that Professor Moore was narrow in his academic creed. He seems to have had a moral compunction about working beyond his strength; what he did he must do well. He was the widowed father of a large and growing family bereft of a mother who had taken much of the care and discipline of the household from his shoulders. His children, three of them boys, claimed a good deal of his time and attention. And he was not one to shirk responsibility.

One thing he continued to do, well into the forties: write poetry. It is sometimes said that Clement C. Moore was a single-poem poet, but such a statement does not show a wide acquaintance with his output of verse. Yet no one may say that in later years he wrote better and better poetry, so far as popular acclaim makes for greatness. There is little trace of development as we note it in so many versifiers. He liked to write "society verse" such as his younger contemporary Fitz-Greene Halleck composed for various social occasions. The second quarter of the nineteenth century knew this poetic form and liked it.

Moore contributed several of his pieces to *The New-York*

Book of Poetry, which appeared in 1837. It was in this volume by native New Yorkers that he first acknowledged his authorship of "A Visit from St. Nicholas." Much of his verse had already been published in newspapers and periodicals. If the Poet of Chelsea had printed "A Visit" earlier he might have saved all who lived after him the trouble of defending him against claimants for the honor of having written the most famous Christmas poem in American literature.

Among the poems by Moore in *The New-York Book of Poetry* is one entitled: "To My Children After Having My Portrait Taken for Them." There are twelve stanzas, each of four lines. The following few will be enough to show their interesting but commonplace quality, though graceful charm is not wanting:

This semblance of your parent's time-worn face
  Is but a sad bequest, my children dear!
Its youth and freshness gone, and in their place
  The lines of care, the track of many a tear!

Amid life's wreck, we struggle to secure
  Some floating fragment from oblivion's wave:
We plant for somewhat that may still endure,
  And snatch at least a shadow from the grave . . .

And 't is the glory of the master's art
  Some radiance of this inward light to find;
Some touch that to his canvas may impart
  A breath, a sparkle of the immortal mind.

Alas! the pencil's noblest power can show
  But some faint shadow of a transient thought,
Some waken'd feeling's momentary glow,
  Some swift impression in its passage caught.

The reader may discern a little more than the trivial in

these stanzas. There is surely a reflection of the poet's sense of irremediable loss in the death of his beloved Eliza, little Emily, and Charity. There is at least the ring of sincerity.

One great service this book of New York poetry rendered was the inspiration it gave the artist, Robert Walter Weir, a drawing instructor at West Point. Weir was a friend of Moore's, but more particularly of Gulian C. Verplanck's. He put the breath of life into St. Nicholas quite independently of Myron King of whom he had very probably never heard. Although Moore knew Weir, he selected Henry Inman, the distinguished portraitist, to paint the "semblance" of his "time-worn face." Inman was a founder of the National Academy of Design.

Professor Moore paid an occasional visit to West Point to see his friends in "Professors' Row." He was fond of the Point; a relative had owned the Academy site and sold it to the government. There were usually a number of celebrities there, among them on one occasion General Winfield Scott and Lt. Simon Buckner, a classmate of Lt. Ulysses S. Grant, to whom he would one day surrender unconditionally.

Weir was a special favorite. He had a studio not far from the house of Professor William Bartlett, whose small daughter used to run over to see the artist making a fat, funny-looking man into a jovial old fellow he called Santa Claus. There was the fireplace she had heard about in "A Visit from St. Nicholas"; and there was the self-same chimney all ready to let Santa mount to the top and drive off with his "eight tiny reindeer." Mr. Weir attached Santa's pipe to the side of his cap and ran his finger "aside of his nose," the poetic for Irving's "beside his nose." Nick is dressed in a brown suit with a red cloak round his shoulders. The face is a joy to see: the furtive glance, smiling cheeks.*

Weir exhibited his "Santa Claus or St. Nicholas" at the

* See Frontispiece for reproduction of the Weir illustration.

National Academy in 1837. A second canvas is today in the New York Historical Society. The figure of St. Nick owes much to Robert Walter Weir but also to Henry M. Onderdonk, friend and onetime neighbor of Moore's when the poet lived in wintertime on lower Broadway. Onderdonk's printing shop was a place to step into for a chat. Theodore C. Boyd engraved the illustrations for "A Visit from St. Nicholas" as "A Present for Good Little Boys and Girls." Boyd used a Dutch handyman named Peter as his model. We should like to know more about this "St. Nick." Was he the Dutch workman whom the Poet of Chelsea fashioned into the immortal figure of his fancy?

To anticipate a little, St. Nick or Santa Claus underwent several revisions as the years passed by. It has been said that Thomas Nast in his "Christmas Drawings for the Human Race" fixed the old fellow for all time. But Nast's Santa was only one and is somewhat unlike our present-day Santa in stature and in costume. The fact is, Santa Claus as we know him is an evolution, so to speak, largely from Weir's. Somehow, the garb has become a flaming red as we see him on every other street corner at Christmastime, ringing his bell to attract youngsters and their elders inside department stores or to induce the passerby to drop a coin in a large box for a welfare organization. "Santalands" under varied names cast a spell on old and young. At one of these, in the Adirondacks, nostalgic adults stand at St. Nick's bedside in awesome respect for childhood's hero. Even Mrs. Santa is at the door. An upstate New York school offers a week's training for the Merry Christmas work of a street-corner Santa Claus and garbs him from head to foot in the more or less standardized colors, so gay and bright, and so familiar now, around the holidays.

In the Library of Congress there are no fewer than forty editions of Moore's poem; many besides are in libraries

A FAMOUS CONCEPTION OF SANTA CLAUS IN 1890

throughout the country. Several editions have been printed in England. American publishers vie with each other across the land, from New York to Wisconsin to California. Wisconsin and New York have taken a particular fancy to "A Visit from St. Nicholas." Every year it is reprinted with fresh drawings and elaborate but appropriate formats. Commercialism has given "A Visit" to books of parodies, none of them during Clement Moore's lifetime, fortunately. The poem has been translated into most of the languages of Europe. It has winged its way across the Andes and to other far places. The blind have it in braille. There must be very few children the world round who do not know what once happened, and can still happen, on the "night before Christmas."

One of Moore's fellow-parishioners told the story of a St. Louis lawyer who was perusing a New York newspaper when he chanced upon the poet's name as the author of "A Visit from St. Nicholas." The item called to mind a wedding in Missouri a long time before. "Wallpaper and whitewash were unknown at the log farmhouse," where the lawyer was staying; the owner had pasted newspapers over the logs. "I remember," he went on, "that I busied myself reading the papers on the walls. One of them contained the poem. I spoke of it to the groom who said that he had been struck by it and had pasted it up in order to preserve it." The parson read the poem to the wedding guests at the reception that followed the service. And it happened to be Christmas Eve!

The odd thing is that Clement Moore had no idea that his "Visit" merited publication until friends prevailed upon him to let the distinguished literary critic, Charles Fenno Hoffman, include it in *The New-York Book of Poetry*. Seven years afterward, in 1844, it appeared again in *Poems* by Clement C. Moore, LL.D. It was dedicated to his "dear children." Prefacing the work with a few words, he explained: "In compliance with your wishes, I here present you with a volume of verses written at different periods of my life. I have not made a selection from among my verses of such as are of any particular cast, but have given you the melancholy and the lively, the serious and the sportive, and even the trifling; such as relate solely to our domestic circle and those of which the subjects take a wide range. We are so constituted that a good honest, hearty laugh, which conceals no malice, and is excited by nothing corrupt, however ungenteel it may be, is healthful to both body and mind; and it is one of the benevolent ordinances of Providence that we are thus capable of these alternations of sorrow and trouble, with mirth and gladness. Another reason why the mere trifles in this volume have not been withheld is that such things have been often found to afford greater pleasure than what was by myself esteemed of more worth."

The controversy over who wrote "A Visit from St. Nicholas" should have been settled when this volume was published. But literary quarrels have a longevity which astonishes any one interested in them. The most serious claimant has been Major Henry Livingston, Jr., not personally but rather through the efforts of Dr. William Livingston Thomas, who toiled for thirty years to establish his grandfather as the undoubted author of Moore's poem. The effort was commendable but futile, thus far at any rate. Better proof will be needed. As of today the problem is not resolved in the Major's favor. In the Appendix, there is a further word on this matter.

There have been, of course, a number of literary discussions of similar character. Every one remembers the mysterious *Letters of Junius* and the disputed poems by Thomas Chatterton, "the marvelous boy," whose suicide at eighteen urged the adventurous to prove the unprovable. In America one of the noteworthy cases centered in "Mary's Little Lamb." The poet, Mrs. Sarah Josepha Hale, editor of *Godey's Lady's Book,* challenged the principal contender with such finality that the young John Roulstone receded into the shadows. The delightful poem is now assured a blissful future free from further molestation.

A subtle criticism of Moore's authorship has come from some literary critics who contend that a man of his temperament, learning, experience, and poetic bent could never have written so jolly a bit of verse as "A Visit from St. Nicholas." But Clement C. Moore was not so learned, so serious-minded a person that he could not enjoy "a bit of fun." He wrote another humorous poem which, while not familiar to most people, clearly indicates that he had a jocular strain not too thin, after all. Here it is in full, with his own prefatory remarks:

The following piece of fun was occasioned by a subject for composition given to the boys of a grammar school [Columbia Grammar School] attended by one of my sons—viz. "which are to be preferred, the pleasures of a pig or a chicken?"

On a warm summer day, in the midst of July,
A lazy young pig lay stretched out in his sty,
Like some of his betters, most solemnly thinking
That the best things on earth are good eating and drinking.
At length, to get rid of the gnats and the flies,
He resolv'd, from his sweet meditations to rise;
And, to keep his skin pleasant, and pliant, and cool,
He plung'd him, forthwith, in the next muddy pool.
When, at last, he thought fit to arouse from his bath,
A conceited young rooster came just in his path:
A precious smart pig, full in vanity drest,

119

Who thought, of all creatures, himself far the best.
"Hey day! little grunter, why where in the world
Are you going so perfum'd, pomatum'd, and curl'd?
Such delicate odors my senses assail,
And I see such a sly looking twist in your tail,
That you, sure, are intent on some elegant sporting;
Hurra! I believe, on my life, you are courting;
And that figure which moves with such exquisite grace,
Combin'd with the charms of that soft-smiling face,
In one who's so neat and adorn'd with such art,
Cannot fail to secure the most obdurate heart.
And much joy do I wish you, both you and your wife,
For the prospect you have of a nice pleasant life."
"Well said, Master Dunghill," cried Pig in a rage.
"You're, doubtless, the prettiest beau of the age,
With those sweet modest eyes staring out of your head,
And those lumps of raw flesh, all so bloody and red.
Mighty graceful you look with those beautiful legs,
Like a squash or a pumpkin on two wooden pegs.
And you've special good reason your own life to vaunt,
And the pleasures of others with insult to taunt;
Among cackling fools, always clucking or crowing,
And looking up this way and that way, so knowing,
And strutting and swelling, or stretching a wing,
To make you admired by each silly thing;
And so full of your own precious self, all the time,
That you think common courtesy almost a crime;
As if all the world was on the lookout
To see a young rooster go scratching about."

Hereupon, a debate, like a whirlwind, arose,
Which seem'd fast approaching to bitings and blows;
'Mid squeaking and grunting, Pig's arguments flowing,
And Chick venting fury 'twixt screaming and crowing.

At length, to decide the affair, 'twas agreed,
That to counsellor Owl they should straightway pro-
    ceed;
While each, in his conscience, no motive could show,
But the laudable wish to exult o'er his foe.
Other birds of all feather, their vigils were keeping,
While Owl, in his nook, was most learnedly sleeping:
For, like a true sage, he preferred the dark night,
When engaged in his work, to the sun's blessed light.
Each stated his plea, and the owl was required
To say whose condition should most be desired.
It seem'd to the judge a strange cause to be put on,
To tell which was better, a fop or a glutton;
Yet, like a good lawyer, he kept a calm face,
And proceeded, by rule, to examine the case;
With both his round eyes gave a deep-meaning wink,
And, extending one talon, he set him to think.
In fine, with a face much inclin'd for a joke,
And a mock solemn accent, the counsellor spoke—
" 'Twixt *Rooster* and *Roaster,* this cause to decide,
Would afford me, my friends, much professional pride.
Were each on the table serv'd up, and well dress'd,
I could easily tell which I fancied the best;
But while both here before me, so lively I see,
This cause is, in truth, too important for me;
Without trouble, however, among human kind,
Many dealers in questions like this you may find,
Yet, one sober truth, ere we part, I would teach—
That the life you each lead is best fitted for each.
'Tis the joy of a cockerel to strut and look big,
And, to wallow in mire, is the bliss of a pig.
But, whose life is more pleasant, when viewed in itself,
Is a question had better be laid on the shelf,
Like many which puzzle deep reasoners' brains,

And reward them with nothing but words for their
  pains.
So now, my good clients, I have been long awake,
And I pray you, in peace, your departure to take.
Let each one enjoy, with content, his own pleasure,
Nor attempt, by himself, other people to measure."

Thus ended the strife, as does many a fight;
Each thought his foe wrong, and his own notions right.
Pig turn'd, with a grunt, to his mire anew,
And He-biddy, laughing, cried *cock-a-doodle-doo.*

"A poet," wrote Wordsworth, a contemporary of Moore's,
"is a man with a more lively sensibility, more enthusiasm
and tenderness, who has a greater knowledge of human
nature, and a more comprehensive soul, than are common
among mankind." No one, we presume, would rank the Poet
of Chelsea with the Poet of Rydal Mount. Nevertheless, it
is possible to see that they had much in common: something of the "lively sensibility," something of the "enthusiasm and tenderness," something of the "comprehensive soul."
There was also a common degree of knowledge of human
nature; in fact, Clement Moore may have been endowed
with as great an insight into the human nature of childhood
as Wordsworth. Certainly, for wide, popular appeal, nothing
written by the Victorian laureate compares with "A Visit
from St. Nicholas." One may not look with an air of intellectual superiority at a character like St. Nick who has endeared himself to generation after generation of the so-
phisticated and unsophisticated alike.

Clement C. Moore appears to have been conscious of his
poetic ability, modest though he always was. In his "Letter
to a Friend," which introduced Duer's translation of Juvenal's satire, he gave us his own ideas on the art of poesy:
"Every admirer of genuine poetry should be anxious to see

preserved all the remains of her ancient dignity. No production which assumes the guise of poetry ought to be tolerated, if it possess no other recommendation than the glow of its expressions and the tinkling of its syllables, or the wanton allurement of the ideas which it conveys. It should be scrupulously required, that whenever words are put together, they be assembled for some rational purpose; that if the affections be addressed, the feeling intended to be excited be one of which human nature is susceptible; that if an image be presented to the imagination, its form be distinguished; that if reason be called upon, something be expressed which the mind can comprehend."

The Chelsea poet tried to follow his own precepts in performance. He did no worse than Wordsworth often did in the famous *Lyrical Ballads*. That Poet Moore did not measure up to Critic Moore is not to be charged to his discredit. Neither did Wordsworth. Try to read through the *Excursion* at a single sitting and you will find yourself skipping many a dreary stretch of poetic Sahara.

We find in Moore's verses not infrequently a meticulous sense for the fitting word, a feeling for the precise rhyme, a sensitive regard for smooth rhythm. While he did not hear the bugle calls of the best in contemporary British poetry he was not altogether inferior to many of America's versifiers. There are haunting lines in Moore as in Poe. There is rarely so infelicitous a rhyming in "The Pig and the Rooster" as occasionally even in Poe's "The Raven"; Moore's "put on" and "glutton" are on a par with "lattice" and "thereat is" in

"Surely," said I, "surely that is something at my window lattice;
Let me see, then, what thereat is and the mystery explore."

But then, as James Russell Lowell said, Poe was only "three-fifths of him genius"—two-fifths were "sheer fudge." We should never be likely to call Clement Moore "sheer fudge," in any proportion, although we might hesitate to say in what degree he was a literary genius such as Poe generally was.

Most important of all, St. Nick comes alive, and is alive forevermore. Few writers across the centuries have created a character of more enduring fame. Lovable and shrewd, hard-working and efficient, yet never really tired, though literally heavy-laden—certainly never tiresome—St. Nick shows not a sign of soul-weariness. There is eternal youth in his kindly, wrinkled old face. Even Rip Van Winkle is not more conspicuous in our literary hall of fame.

For some unknown reason Moore's careful religious upbringing and his Chelsea countryside with its sweeping view of the Hudson and the wooded bluff on which he lived made little poetic impression on him—little to inspire the poet within him. Bryant was no greater moralist than Moore, but he gave the American people the religio-moral satisfaction they craved in a day when McGuffey's *Readers* were the core of the curriculum in most schools. There is nothing in Moore's poetry to put alongside this stanza from "To a Waterfowl":

> He who from zone to zone
> > Guides through the boundless sky thy certain
> > > flight,
> In the long way that I must tread alone,
> > Will lead my steps aright.

Or Francis Scott Key's

> Lord with glowing heart I'd praise thee—
> For the bliss thy love bestows,
> For the pardoning grace that saves me,
> And the peace that from it flows. . . .

Moore was a sociable human being but no one ever charmed him to write such a moving quatrain as this by Halleck in memory of Joseph Rodman Drake:

> Green be the turf above thee,
>   Friend of my better days!
> None knew thee but to love thee,
>   None named thee but to praise.

The Poet of Chelsea loved his country with a sincere devotion but he did not express his patriotism in such stirring verse as Drake's "The American Flag":

> When Freedom, from her mountain height,
>   Unfurled her standard to the air,
> She tore the azure robe of night,
>   And set the stars of glory there.

In his own limited field, however, Clement C. Moore ranks well with Bryant, Key, Halleck, and Drake. He did something which has brought him unwittingly far greater fame. Except Poe, he is better known today, and far better loved, than most of the poets of our early national era.

Moore's taste ran to music almost as much as to poetry. At least once he tried his hand at composition. It was something of a novelty. In 1838 he arranged verses 10 to 18 of familiar Psalm 51, beginning "Create in me a new heart, O Lord," as a Hebrew chant for the seminary commencement held in the Chelsea church. He had little to go by; Hebrew precedent was scant, with only a scattered hint or two in the Bible. But the past few decades had yielded material available for scholars, and, of course, there was a large stock of Hebrew words. There was a book of Psalm settings by Solomon Sulzer, which he may have consulted. Sulzer was a scholarly Austrian cantor. Most important were the Chelsea professor's good ear for rhythm, his deep feeling for the ancient Hebrew tongue.

The commencement congregation must have listened with a sense of novelty, for the Psalms were read responsively at regular services. Moore himself was at the organ to guide his chant through uncharted air waves. There is no record as to his success; if he ever repeated the performance we do not know.

George Templeton Strong, the bright young man on Trinity's vestry, thought he would like to hear Professor Moore at St. Peter's console. Just twenty, Strong had a young friend, Jesse Spencer, who was to be ordained in Chelsea's new church of which his father was Clement Moore's fellow-warden. St. Peter's had set Trinity's gift of the historic old iron railing in front of the edifice on Twentieth Street. We say historic for through its gates when on lower Broadway many a notable had passed: Washington, Hamilton, and others whom every schoolboy knows. It may be that on this last Sunday in June, 1840, young Strong also wished to take a look at the ancient relic in its brownstone bases.

Strong was not in a fit mood to appreciate the Chelsea poet's playing. He arrived very warm and perspiring; the whole musical setting was most disappointing. And such a fine instrument, too—brand new and without an equal in the city! Not even at Trinity! An Erben organ deserved better, indeed, the best. Professor Moore, Strong conceded, might be called "scientific," but he was lacking in the "mechanical department." His background in music was satisfactory, but his instrumentation not so good. All of which was doubtless so in comparison with the expertness of Edward Hodges, a master organist, whom Strong was used to hearing.

Strong says he sweated away two pounds as he came up Broadway on that warm Sunday morning. The church was tolerably full but intolerably hot. Though out of sorts with the weather and Moore's playing, he ventured up to Chelsea again in the cooler evening to hear the newly ordained Rev.

Courtesy of St. Peter's Church, New York

ST. PETER'S CHURCH, CHELSEA, IN 1849

Jesse Ames Spencer preach his first sermon, which was to his liking: so free of humbug and without a bit of affectation. Not a word about Dr. Moore's playing at this service.

New York was music-conscious, some might say music-mad, in the middle years of the last century. The celebrated Ole Bull gave violin recitals at the Apollo Rooms of the Philharmonic Society. His success was so great that P. T. Barnum of circus fame brought Jenny Lind to America to sing and thrill vast numbers at Castle Garden. So far as we know, Clement C. Moore did not go to hear either the Norwegian virtuoso or the Swedish Nightingale.

Grand opera came to the city in the twenties and thirties. It had distinguished sponsorship. Manuel Garcia, brother of the more famous Mme. Malibran, greatest soprano of her day, was at the rebuilt Park Theatre on Nassau Street. He sang the title role of Mozart's *Don Giovanni* to a packed house where a box seat cost $2. The Park was only a step or two from Columbia College, but Clement Moore does not appear to have gone to hear either Mme. Malibran or Signor Garcia, although Uncle William Moore, the well-known physician, shared a box with the Honorable Philip Hone, New York's former Mayor.

In 1833 Lorenzo da Ponte opened his Italian Opera House at Church and Leonard Streets and electrified New York's opera-goers until a disastrous fire destroyed the building and ruined him financially. At eighty-four Da Ponte had failed again. But Lorenzo da Ponte was not a novice at failure or opera. He had suffered a long succession of misadventures. He had collaborated with Mozart in writing librettos for *Le Nozze di Figaro, Don Giovanni,* and *Cosi Fan Tutte.*

Clement Moore had known Lorenzo da Ponte for a good many years. It has been said that they first met at a book store on lower Broadway, very probably at Henry M. Onderdonk's on John Street. The story has it that they were looking over some foreign-language works when they introduced themselves. Thus, very simply, began a friendship all but inexplicable. They had little in common except their scholarly taste for languages. They were different in ancestry, religion, education, and morality. In age they were a generation apart. But Da Ponte had infinite charm which it seems captivated not only Clement C. Moore but other members of the first families of New York as well.

Lorenzo da Ponte was born a Jew in a ghetto in Venice. His father married a Roman Catholic and took himself and his family into that faith. This tanner of Venice then adopted the name of the priest who baptized them. The young Lorenzo studied for the priesthood, but he was either dismissed from the seminary or unfrocked. A "romantic urge" had seized him and made him unfitted for the altar of any church. When the State banished him, he fled to Vienna where, now thirty, he continued his unconventional behavior. Dresden streets saw him with two young ladies who seemed frantically in love with him, if we may believe his own account. A dentist in Vienna was so infuriated with him for poaching on his romantic preserves that, it was said, he doused Lorenzo's gums with nitric acid and made his teeth pay the price. But, toothless though he was, he kept traveling his merry way. He soon made Mozart his friend, the Emperor Joseph II, too, and Casanova, the star Lothario of his time, perhaps of all modern time.

Da Ponte found his way presently to London. There he wrote and talked himself into the highest theatrical circles. He had finesse—there can be no question about that. He had learning; he had sheer "nerve." He had above everything an amazing "gift of the gab" in half a dozen tongues. Drury Lane, not too prudish, could not stand him and told him to go. He did—to America with an unusually sensible wife. To give him his due, Da Ponte was resourceful: he sold books, he went into the grocery business—and failed. In time, he met Clement C. Moore, who did worlds for him. The Chelsea Poet was eager to learn Italian. Da Ponte became his teacher. The class numbered many a bright name and fair: William Cullen Bryant, Fitz-Greene Halleck, Julia Ward Howe, and Moore's favorite cousin, Miss Sarah Ann. It is quite possible that Da Ponte's excellent method—*conversazioni*—influenced Moore's teaching at the seminary.

America—Nancy Grahl da Ponte with Clement C. Moore—worked a miracle on Lorenzo da Ponte. She made a man of him and Moore got him the best job he ever had, a professorship of Italian language and literature at Columbia on a student-fee basis. Lorenzo held this post until his death in the late 1830's. In our day there is a Da Ponte professorship of Italian at the institution of higher learning where he taught.

Da Ponte's funeral at St. Patrick's Cathedral, in Mott Street, was no less interesting than his life. Clement C. Moore walked with the pallbearers, who included Gulian C. Verplanck, Dr. MacNeven, and Dr. Francis, Moore's physician, who had attended the Italian scholar during his last illness. Buried in a small cemetery on the East Side, long since discontinued, Lorenzo da Ponte's grave is today unknown.

When all has been said for or against Lorenzo da Ponte, it should in justice be added that something of rare gold must have been discernible in so strange an enchanter of so many men and women of highest repute. If there had not been, Clement Clarke Moore would never have fallen under his spell.

CHAPTER SEVEN

Retirement, But Not to Idleness

I N 1845, Clement C. Moore resigned from the Chelsea church vestry. The Carey controversy may have had something to do with it; he does not appear to have warmed to the rector who so vigorously opposed the young man's ordination. It is more likely, however, that Professor Moore was feeling the burden he had carried for a decade and a half. Church wardens were responsible for the physical fabric of the parish; its upkeep was largely in their keeping. He was sixty-six; time as well as wisdom to let younger shoulders take their share of the work, and an ever-increasing work it became with the continuing growth of Chelsea. Through the remaining years of his long life he was a faithful member of the parish he had so generously helped "stablish, settle, and strengthen." Sunday after Sunday he might be seen walking with stately step to the left front pew on the west aisle.

Clement Moore kept up his support of the religious life of Chelsea. He gave liberally and frequently to the rector's discretionary fund for the poor. Parochially minded as a rule, he was never so much interested in foreign missions as he was in the needs of the community he knew well. He returned fifty-five pews to the church without a thought of the $17,000 they had cost him while he served as parish agent for pew sales and rentals. He did what he could to reduce the debt of over $60,000. Indeed, if it had not been for his constant care and interest the past hundred years of faithful, quiet service might have been a story untold.

Somehow, Clement Clarke Moore was able to charge the Chelsea atmosphere with a spiritual quality which has not wholly disappeared across the busy, ever-changing century since. There was radiant life on Manhattan's middle west side in his day. Men and women in humble walks moved away, as New Yorkers are wont to do, but many came back from time to time "to see how things were going" and take a look around for "old, familiar faces." Seminarians returned to glance up at the Tower that shaded the street of their earliest pastoral efforts. Dr. Eli Hawley Canfield, an early rector and grandfather of the novelist Dorothy Canfield Fisher, kept a framed picture of St. Peter's on his bedroom wall at his home in Arlington, Vermont. Some years ago, the rectory had an English visitor. He announced himself proudly as the grandson of the Rev. Thomas Pyne, who had delivered the anti-slavery sermon on Thanksgiving Day, 1835. The young man said that he could not leave America without seeing the parish his grandfather had so often and so feelingly spoken of.

Clement Moore expected to have greater peace to do his seminary work now that he had gained a measure of release from parish problems. He was soon aware that such delights are seldom to be had in a bustling city like New York.

As the years took their toll of energy Moore considered retiring from his professorship. In late June 1850, he did so. The trustees made him professor emeritus. At his last commencement he had the pleasure of seeing a young relative, John Wells Moore, and another young man, John Henry

Hopkins, Jr., receive their diplomas. He had left his mark on the school of the prophets. It is not an exaggeration to say that he was the first to encourage higher standards of music at chapel services. It was he who had arranged the sale of St. Peter's "rocking melodeon" to the seminary for $400—it had cost $500. It was also he, not unlikely, who at least helped select the highly skilled first instructor in church music in the middle 1850's. Moore still believed in putting youth forward and, in every instance, he was justified. The year of his death saw the publication of *Carols, Hymns and Songs* from the pen of John Henry Hopkins.

It must have been most pleasant to hear the Bishop of Maine extol his long service, bespeak his "eminent name," his "consecrated learning," "judicial wisdom," and "meek munificence."

"Consecrated learning" had been the key to Clement Clarke Moore's career at Chelsea Square. He never held an administrative post. The deanship rotated yearly among the resident professors. He was not, strictly speaking, a resident professor—only in the beginning years of the seminary did he live in "Old East," and then for a while only. Since he was not a clergyman this may also have been another reason why he did not take his turn with his colleagues. The deep reason may be found in his sure knowledge of himself. He was a rare man: he knew his limitations. Far happier in a library and a lecture room than in an office, he stayed where he belonged.

Formal minutes upon a professor's retirement can be stiff and stuffy—lifeless. Not so the resolutions of November 1850 commemorating Clement C. Moore's almost thirty years as professor and twenty as secretary of the faculty. The words of the Maine prelate were repeated. With a sense of "reverence and gratitude"—"deep reverence and deep gratitude"— the trustees prayed that the retiring professor's long service might receive "the recompense promised to patient continuance in well-doing."

The Daniel Huntington portrait of Clement C. Moore, which hangs on the refectory wall of the seminary today, was painted shortly after his retirement. The choice of the artist was a happy one. Huntington specialized in portraits of men of deep religious feeling and highest moral character, such as he was himself. A copy of this excellent canvas was made a few years ago for the Columbia University Club house and another for the dining room of John Jay Hall on Morningside Heights.

Retirement afforded time and the leisure for entertainments on the high level of artistic excellence, as we should expect. Light concerts were preferred to opera or the formal stage. Only Da Ponte interested Moore in opera, it would seem. The theatre was never of any special interest. The rising tide of drama in the mid-century left the Chelsea scholar cold; apparently, he did not attend any of the many plays of the time. Though great actors were lionized in New York during his active years, he showed no inclination to see the best in art behind the footlights. Britain sent over Junius Brutus Booth, fresh from his success as Richard III at Covent Garden. He packed the Park and National Theatres in New York. When indisposed one evening, his son, Edwin, took his role. Though physically not impressive as his father was, he won immense acclaim. We have not a word about either of them from Clement Moore.

One of Moore's neighbors was Edwin Forrest, who lived on Twenty-second Street. His Othello was a sensation. But, so far as we know, he was not invited to Chelsea House. What was it that kept Clement Moore from seeing so remarkable a performance as Booth's Richard or Forrest's Othello? It is a safe guess that a lingering puritanism had a good deal to do with it. After all, Dr. Moore held his faith

Daniel Huntington portrait, courtesy of the General Theological Seminary
CLEMENT CLARKE MOORE IN 1850

austerely, and with it the strictest of moral codes. He found such an unseemly brawl as took place outside the Astor Place Opera House in 1849 obnoxious in the extreme. The adherents of neighbor Forrest and his rival, the English Macready, did not endear their idols to Chelsea House. To read in the newspapers that the militia had to be called out to quell a riot which Edwin Forrest's jealousy had caused could not be congenial to Moore's mind and irenic spirit.

Ever since he resigned from the vestry Clement Moore had been engaged in a study of the heroic struggle of the Albanians to free themselves from the Ottoman power. He became immersed in the story of Scanderbeg, King of Albania. As he states it: "The high encomiums passed by Dr. Samuel Johnson, in the 22d number of his Rambler, upon Knolles' History of the Turks, induced me to procure that work from England." In reading it, Moore continued, "I was much interested and entertained by the account given of Scanderbeg, the heroic prince of Epira, and great enemy and scourge of the Turks. . . ."

Moore asked his bookseller, possibly Henry Onderdonk, to import any "Life" of George Castriot, surnamed Scanderbeg, which he could find on foreign publishers' lists. In due course, Chelsea House received a small folio volume with the unbelievable title: "The Historie of George Castriot, surnamed Scanderbeg, King of Albania, containing his famous actes, his noble deedes of armes, and memorable victories against the Turks, for the Faith of Christ, Comprised in twelve books by Jacques Lavardin, Lord of Plessis Boorrot, a nobleman of France, translated out of French into English . . . Imprinted for William Ponsonby 1596."

There was no question as to Moore's thoroughness. He studied what was written not only in English and French but also in Latin. He was particularly attracted to *Great Wars betwixt Mahomet and Scanderbeg* by Marinus Barletius. The story of Mahomet had won the attention of American writers like Washington Irving. It is not impossible that Moore had advance notice of *The Lives of Mahomet and His Successors* by the famous author of *The Alhambra* and *Knickerbocker's History*.

Clement Moore seems to have sensed popular taste in what some one has aptly called America's "literary Renaissance." When he tried to moderate scholarship to the general reader's intellectual level, he was not so successful as his friend Irving, his classmate's brother. This should go without saying, and yet Moore went about his task with sense and courage. He was determined to make his *George Castriot, Surnamed Scanderbeg, King of Albania* readable as well as reliable. He does not appear originally to have considered the book his own, but simply a popular revision of Lavardin's capital work. He omitted many of the Frenchman's observations and summarized the long speeches. He deleted the account Lavardin gave of the taking of Constantinople—for the excellent reason, that Castriot had had no part in it. He left out unimportant matters which retarded the story. He modernized the antiquated language of the Ponsonby translation.

As Moore goes along with his revision of this fifteenth-century tale he branches out for himself. A comparison with the original shows how he makes Lavardin and Ponsonby become Clement C. Moore, as it were. Again, as with St. Nick, Moore has a sure grasp of the art of making a character live. George Castriot is a vivid personality as his biographer molds him chapter after chapter. His essential greatness is brought out by a contrast with his bitter enemy, the Sultan Murad II, and by an etching in clear lines of the devotion of the Albanian people to their deliverer.

From the lowly, servile hostage of the Sultan the lad George is led through all the experiences of a Moslem youth.

The scion of the proud House of Castriot receives a title, Iskander Bey, that is, Lord Alexander, and is brought up in the faith of Islam. But when Murad attempts to annex Albania to his empire, it is just too much. At forty years of age, Castriot sees his chance, escapes by various shrewd devices, and sets out to rally his countrymen. He vows that he will never furl his standard until they are freed. He keeps his word. After well-nigh a quarter of a century of warfare he dies at sixty-three and is buried in the Cathedral of St. Nicholas at Lyssa, where his bones are defiled to fashion ornaments for the infamous persons of his former masters.

"Such," Moore eloquently concludes, "were the life and death and posthumous honors of this most extraordinary person; whose single arm may be said to have rescued his country from the dominion of the Turks, and to have preserved its liberty and glory as long as his life was spared."

Perhaps a poet should not write history. For, said Aristotle, "nothing is more philosophical than history." A poet's concern is with general terms; history demands details, concrete instances. Moore tried to be historical and philosophical at the same time. If his English models, here as in poetry, had not been of the eighteenth century, he might have developed a technique and a style to be remembered. If he had kept closer to the King James Bible, which he studied at his mother's knee, he might have left posterity a classic. He started to practice the art of the biographer too late and missed writing a book comparable to Irving's *Columbus*. Longfellow was wiser; he lifted a single episode from Castriot's life and produced his admirable "Scanderbeg," one of the *Tales of a Wayside Inn*, though it is not his best and is overshadowed by "Paul Revere's Ride."

It is not improbable that Clement C. Moore viewed authorship in the light that he once advised his friend, Da Ponte, to look back upon his career: "It seems to me that you are a little too anxious in regard to the memory that you wish to leave behind you. For all that you have already done . . . will be kept in great veneration. . . . This is enough. Do not seek, like Bonaparte, to conquer for yourself all the glory of the world."

Music was better suited to Moore's temperament. He liked to arrange occasional recitals at his home. One evening, a Mrs. Bostwick "sang delightfully"; Madame Szpaczek accompanied her "with great execution." On a visit to his daughter, Mary, at Newport he listened with much pleasure to a German teacher of music as she played her violin. Some of her pupils were at the pianoforte.

The years brought other musical genius to New York. The noted Austrian pianist, Sigismund Thalberg, played to packed houses in Niblo's Garden at Pearl Street and Broadway. The spacious stage, the deep interior, the lofty ceiling made a matchless setting for this series of recitals by the Swiss-born, Vienna-educated, German pianist of world renown. Dr. Moore bought six tickets for ten dollars. The month was February in the late 1850's. He had his own sleigh or a convenient stagecoach at his door. Kip & Brown's "Rip Van Winkle" ran scheduled trips in all seasons from Ninth Avenue and Twenty-third Street to Bowling Green.

Moore did not care particularly for Thalberg. "He is, no doubt, a great player," he mused, "but he did not please me much. The age gets ahead of me." These last six words explain why he disliked so celebrated an artist: "The age gets ahead of me." Clement Moore had been reared to regard scholarship as paramount for truth, even the truth of musical rendition. Thalberg was not a scholar. Moore had been brought up to shun grandiosity. Thalberg gloried in it. He played to the galleries, as we say. Moore would have none of it, and in general disapproval shut his ears to legato unsurpassed, to a singing quality that echoed in many a memory

long afterward. There was a dash, a flourish, which captivated the public but not the musician from Chelsea.

"The age gets ahead of me." Who, advanced in years, has
not felt the same? Younger masters bring new ideas to art.
Though Moore was bored, George Templeton Strong was
thrilled. His youthful enthusiasm was in vivid contrast to
Moore's lack of it. He was of Thalberg's generation. Youth-
like, he found him the greatest and best he had ever heard
except at the Philharmonic. Everything about his recitals
pleased him: the orchestra, the program, the playing. And
yet, the years have favored Moore's maturer judgment. Thalberg is hardly known today except perhaps "within the circle." A story which the late Olin Downes used to tell shows
his position in our time. A French lady, a connoisseur in
music, was asked who was the greater, Liszt or Thalberg.
She replied: "Undoubtedly, Thalberg." "And Liszt?" persisted her questioner. "Ah, Liszt! He is the *only* pianist."

Ever since his marriage Clement Moore had been a trustee
of Columbia. For most of the years he had been clerk of
the trustees. He had never lost his early devotion to his alma
mater. In 1817, he visited Columbia-held lands at Ticonder-
oga and Crown Point and made a report when he returned.
Seven years afterward he was called upon to deliver the
principal address at the seventieth anniversary celebration.
The graduate who had been asked was obliged to decline.
Another instance of Moore's engaging traits: he did not mind
playing second fiddle.

Trustee Moore began his anniversary talk by tactfully
lauding his fellow-alumni on their idea of holding the meeting. Modestly, he expressed regret that the alumnus originally invited had not been able to come. With a shy touch of
humor he remarked that the alumni might have heard remi-
niscences of bygone days in a manner that he himself could
not give them. What a healthful experience for everybody to

foregather and take account of stock, so to speak, comparing what this class or that had accomplished through the years since graduation! He then swung into the body of his Address with a brief contrast between King's in his father's time and Columbia in his own. Going still farther back, to the very beginning: President Samuel Johnson had been the only professor—the whole faculty—in 1754.

When he compared Columbia with foreign universities he was cautiously optimistic while eager to tell the truth. There was no use arguing the question whether alma mater could compete with overseas institutions. She just could not. Literary apparatus, such as a large library, did not exist. Nobody of literary distinction had as yet appeared on the campus. Little did he imagine that his simple verses would one day make him one of the best known literary alumni on the college rolls.

As always, there was an eloquent peroration: "The glitter and pomp of wealth naturally attract the multitude, while the worth of knowledge and wisdom lies hidden from the mass of mankind. But by making literature a badge of honorable distinction, it must inevitably become more attractive to the eyes of men. . . . Whatever tends to draw men together in the bonds of harmony and friendship, is most desirable in this world of jealousy, suspicion, resentment, pride and coldness. . . . " Then, a few last informal words: the earnest hope that the alumni association might conduct the members "to what is of more worth than all the treasures of ancient and modern lore, to the love of our fellow-men, and to the knowledge of ourselves."

There, in one of the few—very few—public talks he ever gave may be seen a plain marker of Clement C. Moore's philosophy of life. It remained the outward and visible sign of his thinking until the final shadows closed in, nearly forty years later.

We have called Clement C. Moore, Dr. Moore from time to time. Columbia had honored him in 1829 with an LL.D. Belated recognition. He was then fifty. Never afterward did he omit the letters from the title page of any of his writings. Throughout his long tenure as clerk he assisted others to academic awards—especially his clerical friends; nearly every rector of his Chelsea church received an honorary doctorate. One strange omission in the list of Moore's friends whom Columbia "delighted to honor" was Lorenzo da Ponte, who owed his chair to the nod of the scholar of Chelsea. Many a man has been given a degree for doing far less than Da Ponte did when he introduced Italian culture to America. It is interesting to note Moore's possible assistance to James Fenimore Cooper, who was made an LL.D. in 1837. A gracious letter from the "American Sir Walter" to Moore is in the university library.

But let no one think that he could get a Columbia award by hinting how nice it would be. Clement Moore did not like intrusion. He did not like being imposed upon. He was pressed by letter after letter. After the announcement in 1843 that a new professorship of the German language and literature had been established, the first privately endowed chair at Columbia, he was pestered by interested sponsors, though the practice was to let the donor name the incumbent. There was not a chance in the world that Trustee Moore would lift his little finger to make anybody the first incumbent of this German language chair.

As a matter of fact, and generally speaking, Clement C. Moore did not exercise any great influence at the college; nor did he try. Curriculum and atmosphere remained virtually the same as they had been since the college was reorganized at the close of the Revolution. It was not until after his death that it was removed from Park Place.

One of a Columbia trustee's duties was to visit classrooms

and attend examinations. It was not obligatory, but Clement
C. Moore took his post seriously as he did everything else in
life. At one examination—it was a warm July 15—he was present and apparently the only one except the students to keep
awake and interested. President Duer busied himself writing
a letter, Professor Anthon read the New York *Herald*. Professor Renwick fell fast asleep, another dozed in the deep,
old-fashioned window seats. One or two students followed
professorial example; others beguiled the tedium by rolling
bits of paper into hard balls and speeding them toward luck-
less, bobbing noses. What else could students who finished
ahead of time do? They were not allowed to leave. How Dr.
Moore could sit through those three hot hours was hard to
understand. As a trustee, he might have got up and gone
home, but duty to Clement C. Moore, as to Wordsworth, was
the "Stern Daughter of the Voice of God." Some thousand
pages of minutes in his copperplate handwriting attest his
devoted trusteeship at Columbia College.

Through all the decades nothing very exciting happened at
trustees' meetings. There was possibly one exception when
his cousin was a candidate for the presidency of the college
in 1842. It must have been a little trying to sit hour after
hour listening to the qualifications of this one and that. It
took all of Moore's placidity to note the opposition of so good
a friend as Philip Hone who favored the Bishop of New York
as first choice and Professor John McVickar as second. The
former Mayor was a good loser, however. When it was finally
announced that Nathaniel Fish Moore had been elected, he
acquiesced with becoming grace and outward pleasure.
Nathaniel Fish Moore had the extra-curricular requirements:
he was an American, he was a layman, he was an alumnus.
The trustees disapproved restoring the earlier clerical influence. The tall, spare, well-balanced Cousin Nathaniel was a
scholar, first and last, and a man to be relied upon to hold to

the *status quo*. In his clear view education must be of the highest and best in ideals and in classical content. He thought, of course, in terms of a select few, and that was all right with everybody else who counted socially in the mid-nineteenth century. Even Phi Beta Kappa did not seem attractive to the Moores, either Cousin Clement or Cousin Nathaniel. Founded in 1776 at the College of William and Mary, this foremost fraternity of scholars had a chapter at Yale within four years, at Harvard within five, but not at Columbia—not until long after Clement Moore's death. But, then, Princeton waited a generation longer. Moore had a greater interest in learning than in its symbol, however honored the key.

Seven years were enough for President Moore. His urbane spirit appealed to faculty and students alike, but he was essentially a scholar as his cousin Clement was. He had had the pleasure of conferring an A.B. on Clement's son William in 1844 and the next year an M.A. Charles King, editor and man of the world in the best sense of the word, was elected president in 1849. The inauguration was a sensation, an excellent public relations job, the first elaborate ceremony of the kind in Columbia history: quite beyond President Moore's simple manner of having things done.

At once, things began to hum. The college must shake off its lethargy. But change takes time. It also causes controversy. King's efforts and methods led to a historic impasse, when James Renwick resigned his professorship in 1853. The president was determined to fill the vacancy with the best man irrespective of his religion or political views. Charles King had the vision to see that if Columbia were to advance beyond the status of a local institution of higher learning it must attract to its faculty the ablest in their fields.

Clement C. Moore found himself in the midst of the most spirited issue in the forty years of his trusteeship. As clerk he must have known pretty much everything that went on before and behind the scenes. But if it were not for the ever-voluble George Templeton Strong we should have very little to relate. For Moore himself, as always, held his peace; his pen as well as his tongue. Young Strong had been elected a trustee in the nick of time, in time at any rate to classify his elderly colleagues as "fogies" and "progressives." When he looked at Moore, nearing seventy-five, he dubbed him a fogy without ado. There sat the Chelsea doctor and scholar at his minutes, placid as could be, with a storm threatening around him. He seldom missed a meeting, but his fame, Strong was perceptive enough to be sure, rested not on punctuality or regularity—rather upon his having written a few verses on St. Nicholas.

When the question of filling the Renwick vacancy came up there developed a sharp split among the trustees. With some it was a matter of finding the best man; with others, finding the best man with the "right" religious "tone"—the tone that had marked Columbia from the beginning. Dr. Oliver Wolcott Gibbs, thirty-two, was the outstanding candidate, popular and learned; he was professor of chemistry at the Free Academy, later the College of the City of New York, now The City College. But he was a Unitarian. His principal rival, Dr. Richard Sears McCulloh, thirty-six, was a Marylander with no religious handicap. Dr. R. Ogden Doremus, only thirty, was a New York chemist; though highly thought of, he withdrew as the campaign grew tense. Clement C. Moore sat silent as at other meetings less dramatic; he was busy making notes for his minutes. He just kept on writing while the others talked. Finally, in April 1854, came the hour of decision. To the surprise of many, "Old Fogy" Moore voted for Oliver Wolcott Gibbs! Or, at any rate, George Templeton Strong's "Gallup Poll" figured it out that way. He had a news sense rather extraordinary. But the conclusion? McCulloh won.

In 1857 Clement Moore resigned as a Columbia trustee after a term distinguished by years, not by fanfare, not by personal gain, but by a sense of duty. The limelight had not attracted him at all. He had served as his conscience instructed him. As in the celebrated Gibbs case, candidates for faculty posts must have character, ability, and show a scrupulous attention to their work. There are letters extant which attest this. Furthermore, he declined to dominate the meetings he attended. Everybody must be heard. President Charles W. Eliot of Harvard once said of Phillips Brooks as an overseer: "In his judgment of character and conduct, he was generous without being weak. He was tolerant of all religious, philosophical and political views and opinions. . . . " So President Charles King might have said of Clement Clarke Moore as a Columbia trustee.

CHAPTER EIGHT

The Squire of Chelsea

CLEMENT CLARKE MOORE's *Diary* has simple charm, that something not easy to define. It is one of the treasured manuscripts of the Low Library of Columbia University. He began it in November 1856 but, as he says himself, "it ought to have been begun at least sixty years ago." At times, this unassuming record of the last seven years of a good man's life yields little beyond the state of the weather; still, on page after page appear brief but priceless items, as in Washington's *Diaries*.

There are no heroics in this *Diary*: no "fine writing," no straining for effect, no self-conscious looking ahead and wondering what posterity will think of this or that. With artless art Clement Moore gives us a portrait of himself that no artist could possibly paint. Here is the man Clement C. Moore, self-drawn, stripped of all titles, all honors. Nobility shines through as light in a Rembrandt etching. It grows as the reader studies it. We are privileged to enter the inner sanctuary of Chelsea House. Not the old house that Molly Clarke built and he enlarged. It is the new five-story house on the southwest corner of Ninth Avenue and Twenty-third Street. A two-family building, it was erected for his daughter Mary as well as for himself.

CLEMENT CLARKE MOORE'S HOUSE AT NEWPORT, RHODE ISLAND

Very little imagination is necessary to sit with the family in these last precious years. As in the past, there is delight in simple living amid rich but not lush surroundings. The red-brick residence stands today after a hundred years. The entrance betrays the earlier loveliness; the graceful staircase guides one's eyes upward. In the days of Moore's occupancy there were a spacious parlor or living room and a dignified drawing room. Water colors were on the walls, and here and there gold-framed, intimate pictures of Father and of soldier relatives. The tall pier glasses that graced the older house were also here. An iron chest took up part of the poet's dressing room. There were two desks, one small, one large, in his bedroom as well as in his library. "Under the stairs" was a closet. A place was reserved for "sundry books and papers." The ponderous glass-fronted bookcases of earlier days still guarded his scholarly works and books by the historian Gibbon, the novelist Richardson, the ecclesiastical expositor Hooker and many others.

Moore foresaw without repining the eventual demolition of his birthplace and the bluff on which it looked out over the river. When the city wished to extend the east bank farther he made no protest. The shallow waters west of what became Tenth Avenue were filled in. "When the streets and avenues about Chelsea were regulated," Dr. Moore tells us with uncomplaining wistfulness, "it was thought advisable, if not absolutely necessary to dig down the whole place, and throw it into the river." Thus passed Molly Clarke's Chelsea House which had stood in dignified aloofness for well-nigh three quarters of a century.

The shock of the death of Margaret, the oldest daughter, had been tempered by the happy marriage of her younger sister Mary to his friend, Dr. Ogden. In 1850, the poet-scholar rented her house on Catherine Street, Newport, but on the same day leased the property at $4,000 for a long term of years. The house stood—it still stands—on land originally bequeathed to historic Newport's Trinity Church. When Mary removed there, her good father's eager trips with her sister, Terry, to see her, gave zest to his life.

Mary seems to have taken a particular fancy to her father's famous poem. In 1855 she presented her husband with a beautiful, hand-printed copy of "A Visit from St. Nicholas," engrossed with ornate Gothic lettering and winter scenes of old Chelsea as she imagined it must have been when she, a little girl of three, awaited Father's return from Washington Market. She depicts St. Nick steering his "eight tiny reindeer" with great gusto: in furious haste he passes round the main entrance of the house to the side door. Outside there is the desolation of winter—snow, leafless trees. It is a bleak, cold sky, with fleeting clouds uncertain whether to stay or just drift over the cheerless landscape. Father's beloved robins have gone south months before.

A year later, a friend asked the poet for a copy of his St. Nicholas verses. He complied—he always found it hard to say "No." He wrote out the whole poem and sent it with a note. Though the copy has been lost, the note may still be read in the files of the New York Public Library. Sometime in 1862 the librarian of the New-York Historical Society inquired if a friend would persuade Dr. Moore to make another copy of "A Visit." Though nearing eighty-three he did as requested in a generally firm, clear hand a little shaky only here and there.* This autographed copy is today a priceless possession of the Society—irrefragable proof that Clement Clarke Moore composed the poem that has delighted generation after generation of boys and girls, and their elders, at Christmastime.

Chelsea remained Moore's home. Here he enjoyed his friends, few now, dwindling in number year by year. He had

* See pages xiv–xvi for reproduction of this copy.

such creature comforts as city water from the reservoir that New York constructed in Egyptian style on Fifth Avenue between Fortieth and Forty-second Streets in 1842. Enterprising citizens had tried to give Chelsea city water long before, from "the rock on Thirteenth Street," but all attempts of the kind failed. There is only one reference to Chelsea's drinking water in the *Diary*. It is as late as January 17, 1857: "Croton water frozen—connection made with next house."

Let us imagine we see the aging scholar-poet in his library at Ninth Avenue and Twenty-third Street. It is late afternoon; he is reading a volume from his own shelves or possibly from the New York Society Library. It may be *The Constitution of the Christian Church. Its Powers and Ministry*, by Richard Whately. The work was published in 1837 when a study of first-century Christianity was moving men to fresh thinking about their religious inheritance. This had been a preoccupation at Chelsea House, from father to son, for almost a century of tumultuous events.

Clement Moore had always relied on Richard Hooker's *Laws of Ecclesiastical Polity* to give him answers to queries about the organization of his Church. John Keble, poet of *The Christian Year*, had recently edited Hooker and, as Keble's readers were aware, he was considered an interpreter of the Oxford Movement. It was inevitable that Clement C. Moore, scholar and churchman that he was, should compare Whately with Hooker, an old standby who had had marked influence upon his life and thought not only religious but political as well. He found much of Hooker's sweet reasonableness in Whately, the same lucidity of mind and clarity of expression, the same strong thesis.

Both theologians, Hooker and Whately, were tolerant men in the Clement Moore sense. Hooker taught the scholar of Chelsea to distinguish between unchangeable natural law and changeable human law, that is, man-made legal sanctions. The unchangeable derived from the eternal, the changeable from the changes and chances of mortal life. It was this concept that underlay the decisions that Moore had to make in the various associations of his long career: in church, in seminary, in Columbia, and elsewhere. Only once, in the memorable and regrettable Pyne case, had he wavered between two opinions; only that once do we feel that he suffered any confusion of thought as to which law he should follow.

Another book that interested Dr. Moore during these years was John Tillotson's *Sermons*. It had been a long time since he gathered his father's sermons into two volumes, but he had never lost interest in this form of literary art. He liked to make notes on sermons he heard; he now enjoyed reading Tillotson's. The discourse on sincerity toward God and man particularly pleased him. He tells us so in his *Diary*. Tillotson's diction revealed the beauty of simplicity, which captivated the Chelsea scholar almost as much as the substance of the sermons. Then, too, the English divine was so practical, so tolerant toward newcomers of various religious denominations: Methodists, Presbyterians, and others such as were gradually coming to Chelsea. Dr. Tillotson had married a niece of Oliver Cromwell's and had cultivated a friendly feeling toward honest men who differed with him. Nor was he a dry-as-dust theologian. And one thing besides: John Tillotson's biblical and patristic studies appealed to a man of Clement Moore's scholarship which covered a lifetime's devotion to the writings not only of the Old Testament but also of the Christian Fathers.

By far the most difficult practical matter that Dr. Moore had to face and solve in these 1850's was the making of his last will and testament. There was his mentally ill sister-in-law to be provided for; there was physically ailing, beloved Clement Jr. to be especially considered in a trust fund. How his father wrestled with this problem! When the will was finished it was long and detailed, but two specifically worded codicils were added five years afterward, in 1860. The bulk of the Chelsea estate was divided into seven parts and bequeathed to his surviving children—three sons and three daughters—and to his granddaughter, the late Margaret's child. The Newport property was devised to Terry. Clement Jr.'s share was left in trust with the executors. Nothing was left to any of the institutions that Moore had fostered during his lifetime. To do so at his death, he probably thought, might seem like setting up a memorial to himself—and that above all things was farthest from his wish.

But we must return to the *Diary* where we have Clement C. Moore at his best. Here is Moore the Generous Hearted, the compassionate Squire of Chelsea. The poor, the lame, the halt, and the blind, literally, found their way to Chelsea House. The money he supplied to his rector as a discretionary fund for the needy never seemed to keep away calls he had to answer, personally. Hardly a day, rarely a week, went by but some one rang his doorbell. It was not so easy as at the old Chelsea House; now, he had often to go downstairs. Once in a while he showed pardonable irritation, as when a man demanded his help with "an air of authority." Clement Moore could be blunt at times—"too much perhaps," he frankly tells us. As usual, he recovered himself, softened, put his hand into his pocket and pulled out a small sum. One day, a beggar refused the small sum he gave him. "I put the money up again, and let him go," runs the *Diary* item.

After tea, of an afternoon—the old English custom carried over to Chelsea—a blind man knocked at the door. It was a loud knock and brought results. Moore gave him $20. Another day, two women called: one of them "as indefatigable a talker as ever I heard." And he knew, for his household had been strongly feminine for years. Other items at random:

"Gave to a pinch'd up man $3 for a ragged school"; $50 to a clergyman; "a dollar to a man who said his father was a Roman and he himself a Frenchman," though he could not speak a word of Italian or French. "Two men, one a presbyterian clergyman, the other an episcopalian . . . got . . . 5 dollars from me . . . I know not for what." A sense of humor lightened things: "One of them said they would stick to me as long as my head was above water!"

For a mid-December evening we read: "that pest Mrs. —— made her appearance. She got ten dollars from me. . . ." In a month "the pest" was back. He lent her $100. Another month passed. She was again at the Chelsea door as if never there before. He declined to see her, wrote her a few lines instead: "Dear Madam, I regret that my obligations are such as to preclude me from attempting to afford you any further relief. Yours respectfully Clement C. Moore." A while later, he received "a lamentable note"—and sent her $10.

Appeals were not all local; occasionally they were from out of town. A poor woman wanted his help to put a sister into an asylum at Claverack, up the Hudson, where the Moores were well acquainted with the family of General Samuel B. Webb, who had stood with Dr. Moore's father when Washington took the oath of office. An old servant of Chelsea House sought admission to the House of Industry.

Moore was generous toward a number of institutions, among them the Orphans' Home, which Hamilton's widow helped found and support, the Association for the Relief of the Poor, and St. Luke's Home for Aged Women. He helped the Deaf and Dumb Asylum where in years ahead Columbia would remove from its historic site downtown. In 1857 he paid a visit to the new location at Madison Avenue and Forty-ninth Street. Mr. Wells was with him.

For some reason Dr. Moore took little or no interest in the idea of a great cathedral in New York. Bishop Hobart had discussed it with Mayor Hone, and both were visitors at Chelsea House. It may be that the whole thing seemed visionary, impractical. Clement C. Moore was far from the traditional professor type, lovable but gullible. Three-score years after the Hobart dream a cathedral did begin to take visible shape on Morningside Heights not far from the third home of Moore's alma mater.

Nor was Moore inclined to assist in the work of the New York Bible and Common Prayer Book Society, which Trinity Church organized with the blessing of his father, then rector. There were three societies with much the same objective. It may have seemed that one was enough. The New York Bible Society, the oldest, was active in the city; the New York Bible and Common Prayer Book Society, in the Episcopal Church; and the American Bible Society in the country at large. Moore had to keep an eye on his benefactions. Though his wealth was some $600,000 in 1855, he had a number of imperative commitments at the moment and for the future. Six of his children were now grown up, and there might be a larger second generation. In a sense he was land-poor; there were long, inactive periods when real estate values were low or, at least, uncertain. Recent neighborhood changes had not helped make Chelsea the court end of town. Tongues very different from English were heard on its streets. The cosmopolitanism so characteristic of New York had moved in on the West Side of Manhattan.

But whatever the shading that circumstances were giving the Chelsea region it was still first in Clement C. Moore's affections. He placed St. Peter's within his care until his life's end. The vestry had shown a lack of harmony of late and the parish reeled under a staggering debt of over $65,000. Mr. Wells came to its rescue and cut down the Robert Lenox mortgage by $8,000. In 1859 he and Dr. Moore suggested a sinking fund to pay off the remaining obligations. Together, with others whose aid they enlisted, they had reduced the total indebtedness to $18,500 by 1860. That year, Mr. Wells died of a stroke and left a lonesome place in Chelsea and particularly at Chelsea House. Clement Moore was as much bereaved as by the death of a close relative.

There is one striking omission as we peruse the *Diary.* Nowhere is there a reference to the stern political drama of the 1850's and 1860's. His mother had plenty to write about to Lady Affleck. Would she have nothing to say now? Nothing on President Buchanan, hobbling today on one foot, tomorrow, on the other? And what of secession? Not a word! And the Emancipation Proclamation? It was issued before Clement C. Moore died. His slaves were freemen; they had been since the all but forgotten proclamation of Governor Daniel D. Tompkins abolished slavery in New York in 1827.

But it would be a mistake to think of Chelsea as remiss in patriotism. Though the Moores were not military at all, there were others who were. One in particular was Charles Roome, president of the Manhattan Gas Light Company, later part of Consolidated Edison Company. Roome organized a home guard of Chelsea men. Later, as Colonel of the 37th Regiment, he distinguished himself at Antietam.

The German philosopher, Immanuel Kant, once observed that there are two universes, both impressive: the universe of the starry heavens and the universe of the moral life. Dr. Moore had been conscious of the moral life all his days, and sensitive to its impulse, but he appears to have been singularly unaware of the skies over Chelsea until these last few years. It is all the more strange since there must have been many a glorious night, free of traffic dust and fumes, free of city lights and distracting sounds. As the years advanced, however, he became interested in simple, star-studded grandeur and jotted down brief reflections such as these: "In the evening, the moon half full, the planets Jupiter and Venus,

all shining in 'cloudless sky,' presenting a heavenly scene."
At another time: "a beautiful evening . . . Tints in the sky
lovely." Professor Bartlett's telescope had fascinated Dr.
Moore at West Point. It now returned to memory, as did
perhaps Bishop Provoost's, which Moore, when younger,
very likely saw at the home of the amateur astronomer who
was his father's friend and predecessor. Like Tennyson,
Clement C. Moore may have regretted that he could not give
another life to science.

One March item reads: "Newton died this day in 1727."
His singling Newton out for special mention puzzles us. It
would seem to signify a closer acquaintance with physics
than anything in Moore's life leads us to expect. Surely, a
man so spiritually minded did not follow Sir Isaac Newton
the full length of his materialistic speculations.

Deaths were many among long-cherished friends. Mayor
Hone, then Mr. Wells, shortly the beloved Cousin Sarah, and
dour but dear old Dr. Wilson, whose house adjoined Chelsea
Church. The rector, Dr. Alfred Baury Beach, was a staunch
prop through these late '50's and early '60's. He had come
from Christ Church, Cooperstown, which Dr. Moore's father
had consecrated in 1808. There were other ties, too, between
them. Dr. Beach had an aristocratic air about him, touched
by a breath of Vermont's freshness. He displayed an innate
scholarly devotion to the best. He was in accord with his distinguished parishioner in many ways. Both saw social change
from the parochial angle. Perhaps it was because they held
different political viewpoints that Dr. Beach abjured politics in his pulpit. He once advised his assistant to be "distant
toward partisanship." During the years of civil strife one
might not see a ripple on the placid waters. The rector was
never known to mention slavery, states' rights, the Union, or
any other of the burning questions of the hour. Parish peace
prevailed, but who shall say the price was not too high?

Dr. Moore's neighbor and legal adviser, Judge Alexander W. Bradford, brought the Squire some good news in April 1862. They had long been friends. The jurist had been surrogate and for a time a vestryman. The Bradford home, like the rectory under Dr. Canfield and Dr. Beach, became a center of cultural influence among Chelsea's intelligentsia. Few neighborhoods in New York could boast so many places for the meeting of minds.

The good news that Judge Bradford brought Chelsea House is not easy to make out from the meagre record we have, but it seems that Moore's father had undertaken to safeguard the welfare of certain of his parishioners. In some way, this had involved him in the partition of the Widow Clarke's property to which he had added sixteen acres in 1789. With the years had come the deaths of all the principals. The case was now come down to this: To what extent does a father's solicitude obligate his son to the heirs concerned? Should the children of the deceased continue to benefit by an original arrangement at law? At long last, the whole issue had been resolved. As Judge Bradford put it, "the long and vexatious litigation" was happily ended. Moore had no need to add a codicil to his last will and testament.

On June 1, 1863, Dr. Moore sailed on a night boat up Long Island Sound. He was on his way to visit Mary and her family at Newport. Some time before he left New York he relieved the Chelsea church of certain restrictions placed upon it by the original deeds to the lots for the parish buildings. On Sunday, as usual, he attended Trinity Church, which was not far from his house. He had been much concerned over Terry's health. She had been suffering from vertigo. He rejoiced when the physician assured him that it was too slight to worry about. But worry he must, for Terry—Maria Theresa —was thirty-six, the same age her mother was at her death. The recollection was poignant.

July fifth was foggy in the forenoon, but the scholar of Chelsea insisted on going to church and receiving communion. His strength was failing; every one could see it. He realized it himself. On the tenth, five days before his eighty-fourth birthday was to be quietly celebrated, he died, with those he greatly loved around him.

The service at Trinity in Newport was marked by the simplicity Clement C. Moore would have wanted. There was a memorial service on the Sunday following. The rector, the Rev. O. S. Prescott, took as his theme: "The Power of the Resurrection." Clement Clarke Moore was central to his thought. "He was a large-minded scholar and an open-handed Christian gentleman . . . ," he observed. "Modest, unpretending, retiring, always a learner, and ever looking out to be taught, he seems to have striven to live only as has been said of one who labored in another sphere, 'to love and to be unknown.' . . . He was content to be overlooked by the world. . . . He did his work for God alone, with a single eye and a pure heart, undisturbed by inimical surroundings and undisturbed by applause, making Christ his only hope, and Heaven his sole aim. . . ."

Interment was in New York, alongside Emily, Eliza, and Charity in the family vault at St. Luke's Church on Hudson Street.

Newspapers had little space for the first citizen of Chelsea, the poet of the heart of childhood everywhere. There was too much to print about Gettysburg and Vicksburg. The war had taken a decisive turn for the Union though draft riots continued to bloody the city's streets and Negroes were hanged from lamp-posts not a mile from Chelsea House.

St. Peter's vestry expressed the sense of loss the parish had sustained. Dr. Moore had been a "steadfast friend and most liberal supporter." His life would be remembered "as exemplary of every Christian virtue." His name would be cher-

Wide World Photo

AT THE GRAVE OF CLEMENT CLARKE MOORE, CHRISTMAS EVE, 1955

ished "in the utmost veneration and gratitude." A marble tablet was ordered placed in the baptistry near the lovely marble font that Clement Moore's friend, the well-known artist, William Sidney Mount, had designed only a few years before. In November 1952, the better part of a century afterward, the poet was still remembered when a bronze plaque was set on the outer north wall of the church tower.

The seminary faculty recognized in their professor emeritus "one whom God had blessed in the selecter gifts; warm hearted in friendship, genial in modesty, instincts, and expressiveness, and of cheerful humor withal; at the same time well accomplished in severer studies, and resolute for more laborious undertakings. . . . " At Christmastime it became the custom for students to entwine holly round the Huntington portrait of Dr. Moore on the refectory wall. And of late, fittingly, the seminary has been erecting Clement C. Moore Hall in his memory.

But we may be sure that Clement Clarke Moore would regard as the best, the highest, of all tributes the simple carol service yearly at his grave in Trinity Church Cemetery on upper Broadway. His body, with the bodies of his loved ones, had been moved here in 1889. Many girls and boys of the Chapel of the Intercession have made a pilgrimage to the revered spot. There, at the western edge of the graveyard, they reverently lay a wreath of winter's green, sing their joyous Christmas hymns, and return indoors where the vicar reads aloud "A Visit from St. Nicholas." With a fine gesture of holiday goodwill the children leave gifts for underprivileged boys and girls in the neighborhood so that every one may say with good old St. Nick:

"Happy Christmas to all, and to all a good night."

Appendices

APPENDIX A

Writings of Clement Clarke Moore

Besides Dr. Moore's various letters and his *Diary*, in manuscript, the following are in print:

1804. *Observations upon Certain Passages in Mr. Jefferson's Notes on Virginia, Which Appear To Have a Tendency to Subvert Religion and Establish a False Philosophy.*

1806. *An Inquiry into the Effects of Our Foreign Carrying Trade upon Agriculture, Population and Morals of the Country.*

1806. *Translation of Prometheus Selection from Aeschylus. In a New Translation with Notes of the Third Satire of Juvenal, to which are added Miscellaneous Poems, Original and Translated; by John Duer.* Letter from C. C. Moore serves as an Introduction.

1807. *A Letter to Samuel Osgood, Esq.*

1809. *A Compendious Lexicon of the Hebrew Language.* 2 vols.

1811. *Translation of a Complete Treatise on Merinos and Other Sheep: Compiled by Alexandre Henri Tessier.*

1813. *A Sketch of Our Political Condition. Addressed to the Citizens of the United States. Without Distinction of Party.*

1818. *A Plain Statement Addressed to the Proprietors of Real Estate in the City and County of New York.*

1823. *A Visit from St. Nicholas.*

1825. *A Lecture Introductory to the Course of Hebrew Instruction.*

1825. *Address Delivered Before the Alumni of Columbia College, on the 4th of May, 1825.* (Facsimile with Introduction by Milton Halsey Thomas, 1940.)

1844. *Poems.*

1850. *George Castriot, Surnamed Scanderbeg, King of Albania.*

Also may be added: *Sermons by Benjamin Moore, D.D.,* 2 vols. 1824.

APPENDIX B

Various Editions of "A Visit from St. Nicholas" in Addition to those Mentioned in the Text

Boyd, Theodore C., (illustrator), "A Visit from St. Nicholas," New York, 1848.

Chase, Joseph Cummings, (illustrator), "The Night Before Christmas." Hodder & Stoughton, London, 1909.

Darby, Ken, "The Night Before Christmas": Set to Music. Solo and piano arranged by Harry Simeone. New York, 1942.

_____. Set to Music. Arranged by Harry Simeone. Choral trans. by Tom Scott. Fred Waring Mixed Voices Chorus Series, New York, 1945.

Darley, Felix Octavius Carr, (illustrator), "The Night Before Christmas." New York, 1862.

Farmer, Edward, (woodcut illustrator), "The Night Before Christmas." San Francisco, 1931.

Ivins, Florence Wyman, (woodcut illustrator), "The Night Before Christmas." Designed by Bruce Rogers. Boston, 1921.

Krehbiel Company, The C. J., "An Historical Sketch of the Origin and Conception of the Poem, 'A Visit from St. Nicholas.'" Cincinnati, 1930.

MacKinstry, Elizabeth, (decorations in color), "The Night Before Christmas." New York, 1928.

"The Night Before Christmas," a Bonnie Book, with two "pop-ups." John Martin's House (Samuel Lowe Company). Kenosha, Wis., 1950.

Ogden, Mary Moore, (illustrator), "A Visit from St. Nicholas." New York, 1855.

Rackham, Arthur, (illustrator), "The Night Before Christmas." London, England, 1921.

Smith, Curtis-Wager, (puzzle picture illustrator), "The Night Before Christmas." Philadelphia, 1907.

Smith, Jessie Willcox, (illustrator), "The Night Before Christmas." Boston, 1912.

Sunday Call, The Newark (N. J.) edition. 8 pages of illustrations with carrier's greetings on cover. Newark, N. J., 1872.

APPENDIX C

The Claims for Henry Livingston, Jr. as the Author of "A Visit from St. Nicholas"

The late Dr. William Livingston Thomas (1871-1941) devoted thirty years in quest of evidence to prove that Henry Livingston, Jr. wrote "The Night Before Christmas," as Dr. Thomas called "A Visit from St. Nicholas." There has been sporadic attention to the problem on the public's part when a newspaper or periodical has played it up from time to time. Such notices have increased in recent years.

Dr. Thomas was sincere, earnest, indefatigable. The results of his efforts merit extended reference. He was born in Poughkeepsie. He was the great-grandson of Henry Livingston, Jr. Educated in medicine at George Washington University, Washington, D. C., he practised for many years in New York City where he rose to eminence in the field of allergy. Dr. Thomas's leisure-time pursuit was historical and genealogical research. Among his activities was his interest in the New-York Historical Society and in the Society of the Order of the Cincinnati. He wrote a number of books on botany, history, and medicine, besides many magazine articles. His major preoccupation, however, was with his family's claims in behalf of their forebear.

The American Livingstons derive from Robert Livingston of Scotland, who established the family in the Hudson River valley in the latter part of the seventeenth century. His estate embraced, roughly, Dutchess and Columbia counties. The two most prominent early Livingstons were William Livingston, Governor of

New Jersey in Revolutionary days, and Robert R. Livingston, distinguished chancellor of New York, the highest judicial post in the state. It was Chancellor Livingston who administered the presidential oath to George Washington at Federal Hall on April 30, 1789; Clement C. Moore's father, the Rev. Benjamin Moore, we recall, participated in a minor role.

Henry Livingston, Jr. was therefore of worthy ancestry. The great-grandson of Robert, first "lord of the manor," he was born in 1748 at "Locust Grove," south of Poughkeepsie. He lived there most of his happy-hearted, pious, and useful life. Not much about his boyhood has survived. Though once a member of a Tory social club before the Revolution, he became a staunch patriot. He suggested "God save the Congress" for "God save the King." In 1775 he joined up with General Richard Montgomery, who had married the beautiful Janet Livingston, and served with him in the ill-fated expedition to annex Canada as the Fourteenth Colony. Henceforth he was Major Livingston. At various times, he served also as justice of the peace, Federal assessor, and city clerk of Poughkeepsie. In brief, he was a man of considerable local distinction, overshadowed, however, by his more glamorous nephew, "Colonel Harry." When Major Livingston died in 1828, his widow penned this moving tribute: ". . . I view my beloved husband as ascended to the Mansions of our dear Redeemer . . . Our *pilgrimage* will soon be over, and through Divine Grace . . . we may all be united never to be separated. . . ."

Major Livingston, it seems, was a dabbler in verse all his days, as many another was in his time. Nevertheless, there is not a word from his own pen upon the authorship of "A Visit from St. Nicholas." No one, outside his family circle, appears to have heard of his having written the poem. Mr. Henry Litchfield West, who has gone into the problem pretty thoroughly, observes that the family's unwillingness to permit their belief of a century's standing to be made known restricted popular interest in Major Livingston until the late Dr. Thomas's day.

Dr. William Stephen Thomas, Dr. W. L. Thomas's son and the present director of the Rochester Museum of Arts and Sciences, now possesses the Henry Livingston Jr. papers. In a letter to me, dated November 13, 1953, he writes that "among the various written family documents" is one in which Jennie Hubbard states quite definitely and unreservedly: "Of course Grandfather Livingston wrote 'The Night Before Christmas.' I believe it just as much as I believe Burns wrote 'Tam O'Shanter.' Father [Charles P. Livingston] knew *when* and *where* he wrote it, and that he *read* it at home before he sent it to be published in a Poughkeepsie paper. Father had the paper carefully preserved, but, alas, I am grieved to say, it is now lost."

Mr. Winthrop P. Tryon, who had access to the Livingston Family Papers and also had the late Dr. Thomas's permission to write an article in *The Christian Science Monitor,* of August 4, 1920, drew attention to a statement by Mr. Sidney Montgomery Livingston in 1900, to the effect that his grandfather at one time owned the original manuscript, which had many corrections.

According to Mr. West, above cited, other members of the Livingston family support Mrs. Hubbard and Mr. Sidney Montgomery Livingston. Some time ago, Mr. Henry Livingston of Babylon, L. I., declared that as long as he could remember, his father maintained that Major Livingston had written the lines generally attributed to Clement C. Moore. The same grandson also said that the verses were first read to the children at the old homestead south of Poughkeepsie, about 1804 or 1805. Mr. Livingston's father, he further stated, had given the original manuscript to another son, Edwin, whose personal effects were destroyed when his sister Susan's house was burned down at Waukesha, Wisconsin, in 1847 or 1848.

Probably the best case for the Livingston claim was made by the late Dr. W. L. Thomas. It appeared in the *Year-Book* of the Dutchess County Historical Society for 1919. He strongly stressed internal evidence. Henry Livingston, Jr.'s manuscript book, he stated, contains 44 metrical compositions, religious, elegiac, satirical, domestic, and social. Unfortunately, the poem in question is not one of the 44.

Dr. Thomas cited the following lines as reflective of "The Night Before Christmas":

> To my dear brother Beekman, I sit down to write;
> Ten minutes past eight and a very cold night;
> Not far from me sits, with her baullancy cap on
> Our very own cousin, Elizabeth Tappan,
> A tighter young sempstress you'd ne'er wish to see
> And she (blessings on her) is sewing for me. . . .
> Now for the news, my sweet fellow, first learn with a sigh
> That matters are carried here gloriously high. . . .
> Now parties to coffee,—then parties at wine,
> Next day all the world with the Major must dine.
> Bounce, all hands to Fishkill must go in a clatter
> To guzzle bahea and destroy bread and butter.

The late Dr. Thomas observed that "Major Livingston liked nature and drew pictures for his children. . . . Some of his verses were printed in the monthly issues of the *New York Magazine and Literary Repository* between the years 1791 and 1794. Occasionally, the poet's original notes refer to his pictures or stories."

In conclusion, Dr. Thomas remarked: "The descendants of this . . . dweller in Dutch Hudson River surroundings are unanimous in their belief in a family tradition taught them from infancy, that Henry Livington, Jr. was the author of the verses beginning with the lines:

> 'T was the night before Christmas, when all through the house,
> Not a creature was stirring, not even a mouse.

. . . A critical comparison of the 'Visit From St. Nicholas' with the acknowledged verses of Henry Livingston adds internal evidence supporting the correctness of the family tradition. . . ."

Director Thomas puts this addendum to the words of his distinguished father: "As you know, the common thought is that the poem first appeared in the Troy *Sentinel*, December 1823 . . . anonymously. However, the Livingston family gave oral testimony and written that it was published considerably before that in a Poughkeepsie paper where so many of Livingston's verses appeared. A fairly careful search was made by my father of all surviving Poughkeepsie newspapers, but he never found it. However, since he searched in the 1920's and 1930's, it is quite possible missing numbers have turned up. . . ."

The W. L. Thomas Papers in the New-York Historical Society yield nothing substantial to support the Livingston family tradition. Though all my life a student of Chelsea, its church, its seminary, and Clement C. Moore, I never heard of Henry Livingston, Jr. as the reputed author of "A Visit from St. Nicholas" until the late rector of Christ Church, Poughkeepsie, Dr. Alexander G. Cummins, sent me an article by the late Helen Wilkinson Reynolds, supporting the Livingston claim. Dr. Cummins asked me for comment. I gave it in a letter which he printed in *The Chronicle,* of Poughkeepsie. I received no replies.

Through these many years nobody else but the family seems to have heard of Major Livingston as the author of the famous verses. Philip Hone, George Templeton Strong, and others gave Moore the credit. Anthologists like Edmund Clarence Stedman, a conservative if ever there was one, have included "A Visit from St. Nicholas" with Clement C. Moore named as the poet. Van Wyck Brooks, eminent critic and literary historian, sees no reason to think that any one else than Moore wrote the verses. Chelsea memories going back to Moore's time have never countenanced any other author of "A Visit."

Let it be added in conclusion that the claims of various localities—Claverack, Sing Sing (Ossining), Newport, and Newtown, L. I.—have been advanced as the birthplace of "A Visit from St. Nicholas." There is not a shred of worthwhile evidence to substantiate the claim of any one of them.

APPENDIX D

Bibliography

The writings of Clement Clarke Moore have been primary in this study of his life and work. The titles and substance of each should be sufficiently clear in the text. Maps and official documents of church, city, and seminary have been consulted; works of Moore's contemporaries have been diligently read whenever they might throw light on Chelsea and its leading family. Letters to and from members of the family have been perused and every extant, available letter of Dr. Moore's studied. His *Diary* has received intense consideration. The John Moore genealogy has been combed for pertinent information.

The following have been helpful, even valuable at times:

Bronson, W. White, *Memoir of the Life of Dr. Bird Wilson.*
Brooks, Van Wyck, *Age of Washington Irving.*
Carter, Henry Clinton, *Historical Notes on St. Peter's Church.*
Cooper, James Fenimore, *Notions of the Americans.*
Da Ponte, Lorenzo, *Mémoire.*
Dawley, Powel Mills, *The Episcopal Church and Its Work.*
Dix, Morgan, *History of the Parish of Trinity Church.*
Ellinwood, Leonard, *The History of American Church Music.*
Francis, John W., *Old New York.*
Gebhard, Elizabeth L., *Parsonage between Two Manors.*
Grove, George, *History of Music and Musicians.*
Hemstreet, Charles, *Story of Manhattan.*
Hodges, Faustina H., *Edward Hodges.*
Hone, Philip, *Diary.*
Hosking, Arthur N., *The Night Before Christmas.*
Irving, Washington, *History of New York . . . by Dietrich Knickerbocker.*
Isham, Samuel, and Cortissoz, Royal, *History of American Painting.*
Janvier, Thomas A., *In Old New York.*
Jones, Charles W., *Knickerbocker Santa Claus.* (Address before the New-York Historical Society.)
July, Robert W., *Essential New Yorker: Gulian C. Verplanck.*
Keep, Austin B., *History of the New York Society Library.*
Krehbiel, Henry E., *Chapters of Opera.*
Lamb, Mary J. R., *History of the City of New York.*
Livingston, Henry, Jr., *Journal* (edited by Gaillard Hunt).

Manross, William W., *A History of the American Episcopal Church*.

New York Genealogical and Biographical Society, *Records*.

New-York Historical Society, The, *Records and Collections*.

Onderdonk, Henry M., *History of the Protestant Episcopal Church in the City of New York*.

Patterson, Samuel White, *Old Chelsea and St. Peter's Church*.

Paulding, James K., *The Book of St. Nicholas*.

Pelletreau, William S., *"The Night Before Christmas": The Poem and Its History*.

Pintard, John, *Letters to His Daughter* (edited by Dorothy C. Barck).

Potter, Eliphalet, *Sermon on David Butler*.

Raesly, E. L., *Portrait of New Netherland*.

Roche, Olin Scott, *Autobiography* (edited by Samuel White Patterson).

Russo, J. L., *Lorenzo da Ponte, Poet and Adventurer*.

St. Mark's Church In-the-Bouwerie, (by vestry).

Smith, Cornelius H., *Centennial History . . . Diocese of New York*.

Strong, George Templeton, *Diary* (edited by Allan Nevins and Milton Halsey Thomas).

Thomas, Milton Halsey, *The Gibbs Affair at Columbia College in 1854* (Ms.).

Thomas, William L., *Papers* (The New-York Historical Society).

Trent, William P., *History of American Literature*.

Trinity Church, New York, *Records*.

Trinity Church, Newport, R. I., *Records*.

Turner, Samuel H., *Autobiography*.

Tuttle, Mrs. H. C., *History of St. Luke's Church*.

Tyler, Moses C., *Literary History of the American Revolution*.

Van Rensselaer, Mrs. Schuyler, *History of the City of New York*.

Walpole, Hugh, *The Green Mirror*.

Weir, Irene, *Robert W. Weir*.

Williams, Stanley, *Washington Irving*.

Wilson, James G., *Memorial History of the City of New York*.

The following articles in newspapers, magazines, yearbooks, and quarterlies have been of value:

Cook, Clarence, "Hamilton's Last Hours." *Century Magazine*, Dec. 1897.

Gilbert, Douglas, "Not Even a Mouse Knows Who Wrote It." *New York World-Telegram and The Sun*, Dec. 22, 1944.

Patterson, Samuel White, " 'A Visit from St. Nicholas': Further Considerations Concerning Its Authorship." *The Chronicle*, March 1943.

Rascoe, Burton, "Who Wrote 'The Night Before Christmas'?" *The American Weekly*, Dec. 21, 1947.

Thomas, William L., "Henry Livingston." *Year-Book of the Dutchess County Historical Society*, 1919.

Thomas, William Stephen, "Who Wrote 'A Visit from St. Nicholas'?" *New York Folklore*.

Tryon, Winthrop Pitt, " 'Twas the Night Before Christmas.' " *The Christian Science Monitor*, Aug. 4, 1920.

Vail, R. W. G., "An Encore for Santa Claus." *New-York Historical Society Quarterly*, XXXV—4.

————— "Santa Claus Visits the Hudson." *New-York Historical Society Quarterly*, XXXV-4.

Walker, Dorothy C., "Christmas House: Chelsea Memories Keep It Young." *New York World-Telegram*, Dec. 21, 1940.

Wall, Alexander J., "St. Nicholas at the Society." *New-York Historical Society Quarterly*, Jan. 1941.

Worden, Helen, "Among People." *New York Herald Tribune*, Dec. 24, 1948.

We are indebted to Hugh Walpole for his description of "5 Rundel Square," London, in *The Green Mirror*. Walpole's father was a professor at the General Theological Seminary before he became Bishop of Edinburgh. Young Hugh relied heavily upon Chelsea tradition about the old Chelsea House.

Index

175

177

179